Beyond
HOME
PLATE

Sports and Entertainment
Steven A. Riess, *Series Editor*

Other titles from Sports and Entertainment

*Abel Kiviat, National Champion: Twentieth-Century
Track & Field and the Melting Pot*
Alan S. Katchen

*Anything for a T-Shirt: Fred Lebow and the New York City
Marathon, the World's Greatest Footrace*
Ron Rubin

Blacks at the Net: Black Achievement in the History of Tennis, Two Volumes
Sundiata Djata

*Fair Dealing and Clean Playing: The Hilldale Club and the Development
of Black Professional Baseball, 1910–1932*
Neil Lanctot

Muscle and Manliness: The Rise of Sport in American Boarding Schools
Axel Bundgaard

My Los Angeles in Black and (Almost) White
Andrew Furman

The New Cathedrals: Politics and Media in the History of Stadium Construction
Robert C. Trumpbour

Shaping College Football: The Transformation of an American Sport, 1919–1930
Raymond Schmidt

*The Sport of Kings and the Kings of Crime: Horse Racing, Politics,
and Organized Crime in New York, 1865–1913*
Steven A. Riess

*Tarnished Rings: The International Olympic Committee
and the Salt Lake City Bid Scandal*
Stephen Wenn, Robert Barney, and Scott Martyn

Beyond
HOME
PLATE

Jackie Robinson
ON LIFE AFTER BASEBALL

Edited by Michael G. Long

Syracuse University Press

Jackie Robinson's columns that previously appeared in the *New York Amsterdam News*,
the *New York Post*, and *Look* magazine are reprinted here with permission.

"Trouble Ahead Needn't Bother You" by Jackie Robinson is reproduced with permission from
Guideposts magazine, Guideposts.org. Copyright © by Guideposts. All rights reserved.

∞ The paper used in this publication meets the minimum requirements of the American
National Standard for Information Sciences—Permanence of Paper for Printed Library Materials,
ANSI Z39.48-1992.

For a listing of books published and distributed by Syracuse University Press,
visit our website at SyracuseUniversityPress.syr.edu.

ISBN: 978-0-8156-1001-4

Library of Congress Cataloging-in-Publication Data
Robinson, Jackie, 1919–1972.
Beyond home plate : Jackie Robinson on life after baseball / edited by Michael G. Long.
pages cm
Includes index.
ISBN 978-0-8156-1001-4 (cloth : alk. paper) 1. Robinson, Jackie, 1919–1972.
2. Baseball players—United States—Biography.   I. Long, Michael G.   II. Title.
GV865.R6A3 2013
796.357092—dc23
[B]   2013002080

Manufactured in the United States of America

For Nate,
who plays T-ball for the Highland Dodgers

and Jackson,
who questions injustice

I won't have it "made" until the most underprivileged Negro in Mississippi can live in equal dignity with anyone else in America.

—JACKIE ROBINSON,
New York Post, August 22, 1960

Michael G. Long is an associate professor of religious studies and peace and conflict studies at Elizabethtown College and the author or editor of several books on civil rights, religion, and politics in midcentury America, including *I Must Resist: Bayard Rustin's Life in Letters* (2012), *Marshalling Justice: The Early Civil Rights Letters of Thurgood Marshall* (2011), and *First Class Citizenship: The Civil Rights Letters of Jackie Robinson* (2007). Long's work has been featured or reviewed in the *New York Times*, the *Washington Post*, the *Los Angeles Times*, the *Boston Globe*, *USA Today*, *Book Forum*, *Ebony/Jet*, and many other newspapers and journals. He has appeared on C-Span and NPR, and his speaking engagements have taken him from the National Archives in Washington, DC, to the Schomberg Center of the New York Public Library in Harlem, and to the City Club of San Diego. He holds a PhD from Emory University in Atlanta and resides in Highland Park, Pennsylvania.

Contents

Acknowledgments

RACHEL ROBINSON deserves my immediate thanks. She kindly granted me permission to publish the material included in this book, met with me to discuss an early version of the manuscript, and suggested points that I had overlooked in my analysis of her husband's public life. Rachel is a smart, caring, professional woman who has worked incredibly hard to advance the legacy of Jackie Robinson. Doing so, she has created her own legacy in ways that have rightly earned the respect and admiration of those individuals who have worked with her. My hope is that her remarkable efforts in helping minority students earn college degrees, and building a Jackie Robinson museum in New York City, will succeed for generations to come.

I have had an all-star team of assistants along the way. Sharon Herr, Karen Hodges, and Alex Hagen-Frederiksen offered excellent help with typing and proofreading. Sharon read the entire manuscript with a red pen in hand, and I am thankful for her amazing attention to detail. Even more important, though, I am grateful for her enduring friendship; she has been the best of friends to me. Good luck to my nephew Alex as he continues his college career. Alex, I am sure that you will succeed at whatever you choose to be and do.

My friend Elaine Benedetti, a gifted freelance writer who really loves her dog, has helped me think through many ideas related to this project and others, and I continue to be indebted to her sharp mind, even as we differ on the question of whether I should be a dog owner.

Syracuse University Press enlisted first-rank individuals to offer critical feedback on the manuscript, and I am grateful for the ways that their suggestions have improved the quality of this book. Special thanks to Mary

Selden Evans for her strong, unwavering support of this project. Jennika Baines has done masterful work in steering the manuscript to publication. Mona Hamlin, Erica Sheftic, and Kelly Balenske also gave valuable support to the project. Many thanks to Annette Wenda for copyediting the manuscript with precision and strengthening its readability.

Thanks, as well, to all those interesting men and women who have attended my talks and interviews about Jackie Robinson. Their feedback has helped me deepen my understanding of Robinson at various points in his career. I have always been especially pleased to chat with those fans who, with tears and laughter, have shared their captivating memories of watching Robinson play at Ebbets Field in Brooklyn. I often wish Jackie were with me so that he could see and hear the positive legacy that he created in the lives of countless everyday people.

There should be a Hall of Fame for librarians and archivists. I am indebted to so many of them, especially Debora Cheney and her colleagues in the News and Microforms Library at Penn State; the entire staff at the Library of Congress in Washington, DC; the microfilm staff at the New York Public Library; and Sylvia Morra and the rest of the staff of High Library at Elizabethtown College.

My gratitude also goes out to owners Al and Sue Pera for letting me write and edit at Cornerstone Coffeehouse in Camp Hill, Pennsylvania. One of their beloved customers, Carmen Finestra, a serious student of baseball history, offered substantive comments on the manuscript. Another customer, Frank Suran, has also been more than helpful—recommending home construction companies, expanding my knowledge of college basketball, and telling me where to spot groundhogs. My pleasure upon hearing his knowledge at the coffee shop is matched only by my delight at seeing the lovely flowers arranged by the remarkably creative Chris Suran.

Elizabethtown College has offered me a wonderful home where I can live out my professional dreams with a healthy dose of academic freedom. Thanks especially to Jeff Long, the chair of the Religious Studies Department, and Fletcher McClellan, the dean of faculty, for the ways they have supported my work throughout my tenure here.

Karin and I have two cool sons—Jack and Nate—and we love them dearly. Thanks to Karin for her commitment to their precious lives. And thanks, Jack and Nate, for letting me teach you about the type of life that Jackie Robinson sacrificed so much for both on and beyond the playing field. I want you to know, too, that the love you offer me sustains me every day of my life.

Introduction

Keeping the Legacy Straight

JACKIE ROBINSON, a hero of the Republican Party? I simply could not believe it, but after surfing my way to GOP.com, I found it—a photograph of a youthful Robinson sporting his baseball uniform on a webpage titled "Heroes." The brief bit of text under the photo was rather flat in its prose: "Not only was he a great athlete, Jackie Robinson was also a great Republican. He campaigned for Richard Nixon's presidential campaign in 1960 and then supported Nelson Rockefeller (R-NY) for the Republican nomination in 1964. Robinson worked as a special assistant in Governor Rockefeller's administration."[1] However uninspiring the text, the point was exceptionally clear: the Republican National Committee was touting Jackie Robinson as an awe-inspiring, all-star Republican, a full-fledged member of its Hall of Fame. But just how accurate is this characterization of Robinson?

There is no question that Robinson was "a great athlete." But that may be understating the point.

Jack Roosevelt Robinson was born in Cairo, Georgia, on January 31, 1919. His parents were sharecroppers who did not get along very well, and when the domestic battles became too much for Jackie's mother to bear, the independent-minded Mallie left the farm behind and moved him and his four older siblings to Pasadena, California. Mallie cleaned homes for a living, and she eventually saved enough to purchase her own family home

---

1. See http://www.gop.com/index.php/issues/heroes/jackie_robinson-1/.

on an all-white block, giving her children as stable a life as possible in a neighborhood marked by racial prejudice.

In spite of the racial discrimination he faced on a daily basis, Jackie began to excel at sports, following in the footsteps of his older brother Matthew, known as "Mack," who would win a silver medal in the 200-meter dash, just behind Jesse Owens, at the 1936 Olympic Games in Berlin. Two years after Mack's remarkable run, Jackie earned his own recognition at Pasadena Junior College, where his baseball playing won him the region's Most Valuable Player Award. Jackie's success caught the attention of the coaches at the University of California, Los Angeles (UCLA), and after enrolling there, Robinson went on to become the school's first student to win letters in four varsity sports (baseball, football, basketball, and track), even being named an All-American football player in 1941. It was a historic accomplishment.

Robinson did not graduate from UCLA, and following a short stint playing semiprofessional football for the Honolulu Bears, he served in the US Army. As fierce as his mother, Robinson faced a court-martial after protesting a decision related to his refusal to move to the back of a Jim Crow bus, and after he was acquitted of the charges and received an honorable discharge, he signed a contract with the Kansas City Monarchs of the Negro Baseball League, playing well enough that Branch Rickey, the general manager of the Brooklyn Dodgers, sat up and took notice. Driven by his business sense, his Methodist faith, and his American belief in equality, Rickey had long laid plans to integrate Major League Baseball. And attracted to both Robinson's character and abilities, Rickey targeted Jackie as the best candidate to help fulfill his dream of an integrated baseball league.

Robinson met Rickey in his Brooklyn office, with its heavy smell of countless smoked cigars, and the Dodgers manager told Robinson he would have to "turn the other cheek" if the two of them were to succeed at the grand experiment of integrating baseball. Robinson understood the terms, signed a letter of agreement that bound him to the Brooklyn Dodgers, and began his stint with the organization by playing for the Montreal Royals, their top farm team, in 1945. In his first year of play he earned a .349 batting average and a .985 fielding percentage—figures so stellar that Rickey promptly promoted him to the Dodgers.

The year 1889 was the last time an African American had played Major League Baseball, and Robinson knew all too well, when he starred in his debut game with the Dodgers on April 15, 1947, that he would encounter racial prejudice and harassment on and off the field. That is exactly what happened. Throughout his career, Robinson faced racist taunts from fans, players, and coaches, especially Ben Chapman, manager of the Philadelphia Phillies, who loudly led his team in harassing Robinson from the dugout. But in spite of the racism, and with support from courageous players like southerner Pee Wee Reese, his beloved Dodgers teammate, Robinson excelled in his first year in professional baseball, leading the National League in stolen bases and even receiving the Rookie of the Year Award. Not quite ten years later, at the time of his retirement, Robinson had not only endured countless more examples of racism but also earned a remarkable .311 career batting average and helped to lead the Brooklyn Dodgers to six National League pennants and one World Series championship.

Yes, it is true, as GOP.com suggests, that Robinson was "a great athlete." It is far more accurate, however, to state that he was a Hall of Fame baseball player and one of the greatest all-around athletes in US history—in spite of odds stacked against him simply because of the color of his skin.

After retiring from baseball, Robinson accepted the position of vice president of personnel at Chock Full o' Nuts, a chain of coffee shops owned by William Black and staffed mostly by African Americans. His retirement from the Major Leagues reflected a variety of factors: his testy relationship with Walter O'Malley (owner of the Dodgers), his diminishing athletic abilities, his ongoing frustration with racism in professional baseball (the Philadelphia Phillies, the Detroit Tigers, and the Boston Red Sox were still all white), his plan to become a successful businessman and a hands-on father, and his fervent hope to help the NAACP and the emerging civil rights movement begun by Martin Luther King Jr. and others a few years earlier.

His retirement years, as GOP.com rightly suggests, were also marked by his involvement with politics. But to characterize Robinson as a hero of the Republican Party is to make a claim that goes far beyond the historical evidence.

Yes, it is true that throughout the 1950s Robinson was convinced that the Republican Party—the party of Abraham Lincoln—was slanted toward freedom and that African Americans would do well to avoid becoming captive to just one political party, especially the Democratic Party, with its Dixiecrats chairing key congressional committees. But Robinson was a registered independent in the 1950s.

Nevertheless, as a tireless advocate of "the two-party system," Robinson shocked many of his African American friends when he signed up to campaign full-time for Richard Nixon during the 1960 presidential election.[2] The baseball great was disgusted by John Kennedy's open courtship of southern governors and also quite taken by Nixon's racially progressive statements, his trip to Africa, his work on the civil rights legislation of 1957, and his expressed commitment to move faster than President Eisenhower on civil rights.

But Nixon's campaign proved to be equally troubling, and Robinson soured on the team for going far out of its way to avoid Harlem and other key African American areas during campaign tours. Nixon did not escape Robinson's fierce wrath, either. In October Robinson had lobbied hard for the candidate to telephone his concern to Martin Luther King Jr., who had just begun to serve a potentially life-threatening sentence of four months of hard labor at Reidsville State Prison in Georgia. But Nixon declined, stating that contacting King would have been "grandstanding."[3] John Kennedy, by contrast, telephoned Coretta Scott King, and his brother Robert intervened with a local judge to help secure King's release. Predictably, a grateful father, Martin Luther King Sr., then announced to the press that he would cast his vote for John Kennedy, and the significant bloc of African American voters followed suit, ensuring victory for the Massachusetts liberal.

Robinson was deflated, and just after the election he poured out his frustration in a letter to Albert Hermann, campaign director of the Republican National Committee. "I was terribly disappointed over the election

2. This phrase occurs in numerous letters and columns that Robinson authored. It points to his ideal political society—one in which African Americans would be heavily courted by both parties in every major election.

3. Robinson quoting Nixon. See Arnold Rampersad, *Jackie Robinson: A Biography* (New York: Ballantine Books, 1990), 351.

and feel we are at a great loss," he wrote. "I cannot help but feel we must work for a two-party system as far as the Negro is concerned." Hermann later thanked Robinson for his words, adding this optimistic note: "Personally, it is my judgment that you could be a 'Messiah' for the Republican Party in the days ahead."[4]

Robinson certainly tried to fulfill that role. In the following year, for instance, he implored Nixon to do something about Barry Goldwater's statement to a group of influential Republican leaders in Atlanta. "We're not going to get the Negro vote as a bloc in 1964 and 1968, so we ought to go hunting where the ducks are," Goldwater had said.[5] That divisive statement, Robinson wrote Nixon, "will be Republican policy until someone other than Goldwater vigorously denies that the Republican Party is not interested in the Negro vote." Predictably, Nixon did not distance himself from Goldwater on this point, and Robinson's disappointment only deepened when the Republicans nominated Goldwater for president in 1964. "His candidacy," Robinson wrote, "reeks with prejudice and bigotry."[6] Warning that Republicans were forming a "white man's party," Robinson then campaigned for Lyndon Johnson in 1964.[7]

But he drifted back to the Republican fold once again in the mid-1960s, this time focusing his lobbying efforts on his all-time favorite politician, Republican governor Nelson Rockefeller of New York. "The sooner

4. Letter from Robinson to Albert Hermann, November 18, 1960, Jackie Robinson Papers (JRP), box 5, folder 19, Library of Congress (LOC), Washington, DC; letter from Albert Hermann to Robinson, November 23, 1960, JRP, box 5, folder 19.

5. Quoted in Pearl T. Robinson, "Whither the Future of Blacks in the Republican Party?," *Political Science Quarterly* 97, no. 2 (1982): 214. Part of the quotation can also be found in "Goldwater Solicits G.O.P. Votes for Southern Segregationists," *New York Times* (NYT), November 19, 1961, 70.

6. Letter from Robinson to Richard Nixon, December 8, 1961, Richard M. Nixon Papers (RMNP), general correspondence, series 320, box 649; JRP, box 5, folder 11, Richard M. Nixon Library, Anaheim, California; letter from Robinson to Nelson Rockefeller, October 7, 1964, Nelson A. Rockefeller Papers (NAR) Personal, RG 4, series L, box 207, folder 2078, Rockefeller Family Archives, Rockefeller Archive Center, Sleepy Hollow, New York.

7. See, for instance, Jackie Robinson, "The G.O.P.: For White Men Only?," *Saturday Evening Post*, August 10–17, 1963, 10, 12.

there is a strong two-party system in New York as well as nationwide, the sooner we get our rights," he penned Rockefeller in 1965.[8] And with Robinson's help—Jackie served as special assistant to the governor for community affairs—Rockefeller built a solid base of African American voters in New York.

But the party faithful on the national level never warmed up to the (relatively) liberal Rockefeller, and Robinson's hope for a two-party system fizzled yet again when Nixon saddled up to southern segregationists during the 1968 presidential election, leaving Robinson to wonder how any self-respecting African American could ever vote for the "racist" Republican ticket.[9] In one of his blunter moments, he even stated that the GOP could go to hell.

Unbelievably, though, Robinson refused to surrender. Still arguing that "it is not good policy for any minority to put all of their eggs in one political basket," and concerned about the possibility of a Democratic peacenik becoming president, he attended a 1972 dinner hosted by the Black Committee to Reelect the President (BCREEP).[10] But this daunting loyalty proved, once again, to be a fruitless venture, at least in terms of advancing the civil rights agenda among top Republicans. In the spring of that same year—the year of Robinson's death—Nixon called for a moratorium on busing designed to achieve racial balance in public schools.

No matter what the Republican Party's website might claim today, then, Jackie Robinson never became an all-star among the party base and its leaders, and the reason for his failure is strikingly clear: Republican leaders in the late 1960s and 1970s confined him to the corner of the dugout so that they could please the millions of white fans who were loudly cheering for political order, not racial justice, in those turbulent times of white backlash against the civil rights movement.

8. Letter from Jackie Robinson to Nelson Rockefeller, February 22, 1965, NAR Personal, RG 4, series J.2, box 52, folder 326.

9. "Jackie Robinson Splits with G.O.P. over Nixon Choice," *NYT*, August 12, 1968, 1.

10. Letter from Robinson to Richard Nixon, n.d. [December 1971], quoted in Jackie Robinson, *I Never Had It Made* (1972; reprint, New York: Ecco/HarperCollins, 1995), 242–43.

At the end of his life, Robinson was left to plead. "Because I want so much to be a part of and to love this nation as I once did," he wrote in his last letter to Nixon, "I hope you will take another look at where we are going and be the president who leads the nation to accept difficult but necessary action, rather than one who fosters division."[11] Nixon did not reply, and forty years later the silence is still deafening—especially when one notices that a photograph of Barry Goldwater appears in the same "Heroes" section of the GOP website.

Nevertheless, Robinson does not belong on the Democrats' website, either. As just alluded to, although he campaigned for Hubert Humphrey in the 1960 Democratic race, he could not stomach backing the nominee, primarily because he felt that John Kennedy did not understand African American concerns. Robinson was especially disappointed when the Massachusetts senator did not make eye contact with him during a specially arranged meeting at the Georgetown home of Democratic operative Chester Bowles. Jackie also criticized the selection of Lyndon Johnson as Kennedy's running mate, suggesting that the choice was a blatant appeal to southern segregationists. But Robinson then backed Johnson in 1964, finding the new president's action on civil rights to be especially impressive. Jackie then campaigned for Humphrey again in 1968, but mostly because his favorite candidate, Nelson Rockefeller, had failed miserably at the polls. Indeed, while he favored the civil rights policies of progressive Democrats like Humphrey, Robinson was always more inclined to side with Republicans like Rockefeller on issues related to business, foreign policy, and other social concerns. Add in Robinson's ongoing sense that the Democratic Party continued to give safe shelter to racist Dixiecrats, and it is easy to understand that Robinson was no Democratic cheerleader.

Robinson was really his *own* man—his own *black* man—and he was dedicated not to any one party, or any one politician, but to a cause that was near and dear to his heart: first-class citizenship for African Americans

11. Letter from Robinson to Richard Nixon, March 21, 1972, RMNP, White House Central File, GEN HU 2, box 7.

and other minorities long banished from the white corridors of power in Congress and the White House and on Wall Street and Main Street.

And so, if I may be as blunt as Robinson was, I believe that the GOP has hijacked Robinson's legacy for its own (unclear) purposes. This phenomenon is not new, of course; nor is it unique to the Republican Party. Individuals and institutions have long hijacked the legacy of famous deceased individuals in order to serve and advance their own special interests. Just consider the use of Jesus or Muhammad by opposing parties in the so-called War on Terror.

Unfortunately, those individuals who have passed before us cannot defend themselves against the use and abuse of their legacies—at least usually. But one of the best parts about the legacy of Jackie Robinson is that he left behind millions of words—in letters, interviews, newspapers, television shows, radio programs, speeches, and even sermons. Words that address so many topics—everything from little children at Christmastime to H. Rap Brown in the Age of Black Power. Words that come from the heart—passionate and compassionate, profound and provocative. And words that we can, and should, use to correct those special interests that use his legacy unfairly.

One of the words I just used—*provocative*—points to part of Robinson's historical record, his letters and newspaper columns. In *First Class Citizenship: The Civil Rights Letters of Jackie Robinson*, I compiled, edited, and introduced correspondence between Robinson and major public figures—letters that revealed Robinson charting his own course, offering support to Democrats and to Republicans, questioning the motivations of civil rights leaders, and challenging the nation's political leaders when he felt they were guilty of hypocrisy. Had the GOP public relations team read any of Robinson's civil rights letters, it would have discovered just how wrong it was even to entertain the image of Robinson as a GOP hero. Or had the team researched the opinions that Robinson expressed so clearly, and thrillingly, in his many newspaper columns, it would have reached a similar conclusion—even though his columns are significantly different from his civil rights letters.

Robinson wrote his columns for two different media outlets—for the *New York Post* from 1959 to 1960 and for the *New York Amsterdam News* from 1962 to 1968—and both offered him national syndication. In his announcement of Robinson's new column, *Post* editor James Wechsler stated: "I believe this is the first time that real national syndication has been attempted for a columnist who happens to be a Negro. But I am confident that he will find a wide audience."[12] Although Wechsler's history was a bit shortsighted—African American newspapers already had syndicated columnists in print—he was right that it was the first time that a newspaper owned and run by whites syndicated an African American columnist, thus making Robinson another "first" in professions long dominated by whites.

It may seem strange to us now that Robinson found a home at the *Post*, but at this point in history the newspaper was known for its liberalism. It was simply impossible to find the politically conservative opinions that are so characteristic of its op-ed pages today. And as a liberal paper, the *Post* had given Robinson, and larger civil rights issues, favorable coverage through the years; it was one of the few racially progressive media outlets of its time.

It was more than the "first" that Wechsler extolled for his readers. "Robinson," he added, "is an intelligent, independent, and articulate human being who follows no party line. He has strong feelings on many subjects and I think many people will be interested in reading what he has to say." Wechsler was no doubt right on this last point. Jackie Robinson was a national icon—a hero—and the editor well knew that he could possibly expand readership, especially among blacks, by having Robinson in his pages. Hiring Jackie was smart business.

Wechsler was also dead-on about Robinson's "strong feelings." Jackie Robinson held deeply passionate feelings—including a burning need to speak his mind in public forums, about whatever subject captured his attention, and in a way that would leave no one wondering what his true feelings were on a particular issue. He made this same point remarkably clear in his first column for the *Post*. "I've always tried to give as honest and sincere an opinion as I could," he wrote. "Unfortunately, some people

12. James Wechsler, "A New Column on All Subjects: Jackie Robinson to Write for the *Post*," *New York Post* (NYP), April 24, 1959, 96.

don't always appreciate this. Still, for better or worse, I've always thought it more important to take an intelligent and forthright stand on worthwhile questions than to worry about what some people might think."[13]

Why did he agree to a column? In 1959 Robinson was gainfully employed as a vice president of personnel at Chock Full o' Nuts in New York City. But however comfortable it was, the salary of his new corporate job never satisfied Robinson's inner drive and overall mission in life, and he identified two interrelated reasons for undertaking a column—one relating to his success in life and another to his race:

> I've had perhaps more than my share of the good things of life. I'm thankful for this, but it doesn't for one moment mean that I don't share and identify with the very real problems of others. It would be easier, perhaps, just to go ahead and enjoy life and take no interest in politics, or juvenile delinquency, or race relations, or world affairs. In fact, I've sometimes been told: "Jack, if only you'd kept your mouth shut, you'd have won even more honors than you have!"
>
> Well, I think honors are fine. But if having any honor ever means being obligated to giving up self-respect, you can be assured I know it's not worth it.
>
> I firmly believe that because I have been so fortunate it is my duty to speak up where and when I can. . . .
>
> And, too, as a Negro, I could hardly ignore this rare opportunity for one of us to speak to so wide an audience concerning just what we feel and think. That this person happens to be me isn't important. The fact that it is happening is the thing.[14]

Of course, there might have been other reasons that Robinson did not mention—like the chance to satisfy an egotistic craving to be in the public eye—but shaping public opinion on important issues was always an essential part of Robinson's own understanding of his vocation.

---

13. *NYP*, April 28, 1959. Robinson's column throughout his tenure with the *Post* was titled "Jackie Robinson."

14. Ibid.

Perhaps the most interesting feature of the agreement between Robinson and the newspapers he wrote for was that he was free to write about any subject of his choosing; he was not restricted to baseball. And Robinson took full advantage of this freedom, speaking his mind about everything from playing Santa to encountering racism in the Red Sox Nation; from loving his wife, Rachel, to despising Barry Goldwater; from listening to Muhammad Ali's verbosity to teaching Little Leaguers how to lose well. To be sure, as the lopsided size of the following chapters suggest, Robinson had much more to say on certain subjects (like sports) rather than others (like family). It is nevertheless remarkable that Robinson felt free enough to comment not just on professional baseball but also on such things as interracial marriages, suntan lotion, and a carpetbagging Robert Kennedy.

If the range of his topics was breathtaking, so was the provocative nature of his opinions. Although he clearly had professional help writing his columns—playwright William Branch helped him at the *Post* and media expert Al Duckett at the *Amsterdam News*—Robinson made absolutely sure that his voice was front and center in the end result. And without fail his voice was captivating. The columns of Jackie Robinson were provocative in a way that his private letters to civil rights leaders and politicians were not. Like his private letters, his columns were (and still are) strikingly open, honest, and revealing, but unlike the letters, his columns were also written for the masses—everyday citizens wondering what in the world their baseball hero had to say about newsworthy issues and events—and with the hope of increasing the number of readers. Robinson wrote to prod and provoke, inflame and infuriate, and sway and persuade, as he sought to build his readership. Indeed, as Robinson played to win, he also strove to win the arguments of his day.

With their pointed opinions, his columns reveal that the mature Robinson was far different from the second baseman who smiled his way through racist jeers and taunts from 1947 to 1949—the years Branch Rickey counseled him to "turn the other cheek." The Jackie Robinson who appears full-statured in these columns was an African American whose anger at injustice, especially racial discrimination, had a very low boiling point. And, as Robinson himself knew, that fact did not sit well with everyone. Some of his readers far preferred the young ballplayer who did not strike back, or who focused merely on winning the pennant, over the brash columnist. Consequently, more than a few times Robinson's detractors wrote replies that began with something like this: "You used to be my hero, but now you have gone too far afield."

There is also something utterly fascinating that his columns reveal in a way that his civil rights letters do not—Jackie Robinson's tenderheartedness. In most of his extensive letters to political leaders from Dwight Eisenhower to John Kennedy, from Barry Goldwater to Hubert Humphrey, from Nelson Rockefeller to Adam Clayton Powell Jr., Robinson made hard-hitting points about racial violence, voting rights, social welfare policies, busing, and virtually every other major civil rights issue. By contrast, Robinson's columns move beyond the pointed tone of his letters to give us profound insight into the warmth and tenderness that his family and friends encountered—and felt—on a daily basis.

My book on his civil rights letters led me to conclude that by the end of his life, Jackie Robinson was a very frustrated, and impatient, black prophet who railed against second-class citizenship whenever anyone dared to stand in his way. I still believe that characterization is accurate, especially when I consider the ways in which Robinson's diabetes seemed to give him an overriding sense of immediacy and urgency when thinking about injustice in the last seven or eight years of his life. But this depiction of Robinson simply does not tell the whole story that the columns tell. The whole story, as revealed in his commentary, is that Jackie Robinson had a heart full of passion and compassion.

In his various columns we see not just the outraged American prophet who appears time and again in his civil rights letters but also a devoted husband loving his wife with more passion than most of us can ever dream of mustering. We experience a tenderhearted father worrying about the direction of his children's lives. We listen to a son feeling so indebted to his mother that he publicly recounts her sacrifice time and again when reflecting on his own success. We watch a friend going to bat after he learns about racial discrimination against his African American friends on the golf course. We hear a community leader speaking "heart to heart" with young folks attracted to violence. We encounter a stranger practicing hospitality, reaching out in compassion to those persons who were far less privileged than he was. Jackie Robinson, it turns out, had a huge heart—full of passion for the people he loved and compassion for the people he found oppressed. *This* is the Jackie Robinson that his family and friends knew and loved. Indeed, this is the man that Rachel Robinson does not want us to overlook as we tend to his legacy.

Unfortunately, this part of Robinson has not always been visible to the public eye. The media of his day focused quite a bit on his temper on the baseball diamond, missing all the time he spent with children in community centers, with his own children on the frozen lake next to their home in Stamford, or with friends across the country. And since his life ended in 1972, our culture has obsessed on the young ballplayer of 1947—not the man whose capacity for enduring love and friendship was far more than a tolerant smile.

If we are to get the legacy of Jackie Robinson right, it is not enough to focus on the cheek-turning second baseman of 1947, or the all-star player from 1948 to 1956 whose temper could flare, or even the American prophet that he became from 1957 to 1972. Grasping the whole Jackie Robinson calls for us to focus also on his determined love for his family, his friends, and those persons deemed second-class or even third- and fourth-class citizens.

With this important goal in mind, thanks in part to Rachel Robinson's insistence in my conversations with her, I have made sure to compile, order, and balance the book in a way that tends to Robinson's big heart before the reader encounters his strong forearm in politics. I do so not merely to draw attention to the part of his personality most overlooked but also to help the reader realize that Robinson's public criticisms in the field of politics have a starting point in his love of the good life, a life in which family, friends, and strangers come together to help one another build lives marked by love and equal justice.

But it was not his tenderness that got him into trouble. On November 4, 1960—Election Day—*Post* editor James Wechsler informed Robinson that he and owner Dorothy Schiff had decided not to resume his column.(Robinson had taken a leave of absence to serve on Richard Nixon's campaign team in September 1960.) Wechsler, a Kennedy supporter, apparently felt that Robinson's pro-Nixon sentiments had led to unfair reporting during the presidential campaign and that William Branch's writing did not clearly reflect Robinson's personality.

Robinson grew livid, and he thought Wechsler was flat-out wrong on both points—and dishonest in stating these reasons for firing him. True to form, then, Robinson publicly criticized Wechsler and Schiff in his very first column for the *New York Amsterdam News* (January 6, 1962). The pointed criticism smacked of sour grapes, but it also reflected and respected his new African American readership:

> Not too long before I was let go, I had been a luncheon guest of both the publisher and the editor. We discussed the Jackie Robinson column and both Mrs. Schiff and Mr. Wechsler told me how pleased they were with the column and indicated that it was very well received by the public.
>
> No one will ever convince me that the *Post* acted in an honest manner. I believe the simple truth is that they became somewhat alarmed when they realized that I really meant to write what I believed. There is a peculiar parallel between some of our great Northern "liberals" and some of our outstanding Southern liberals.
>
> Some of the people in both classes share the deep-seated convictions that only their convictions can possibly be the right ones. They both inevitably say the same thing: "We know the Negro and what is best for him."[15]

Robinson went on to express his gratitude to C. B. Powell, the publisher of the *Amsterdam News*, and to executive editor Jimmy Hicks, and just to clarify the matter, he added: "Dr. Powell and Mr. Hicks are well aware of the fact that this column will not always reflect the opinions of the *Amsterdam News*. They are well aware of the fact that we will write here exactly the way we feel on any issue."

No one would silence Jackie Robinson.

15. *New York Amsterdam News* (NYAN), January 6, 1962, 9. Robinson's column for NYAN was first titled "Jackie Robinson Says," but quickly changed to "Home Plate."

Even after the *Amsterdam News* dropped his column in 1968,[16] he continued to write letters to the editor, make speeches across the country, and offer interviews to newspapers and magazines and radio and television shows. Robinson *had* to speak his mind—he just had to. But it is also very clear that the public *wanted* to hear from Jackie Robinson. There was an excellent reason lying behind all those columns and interviews offered by Robinson—the public's insatiable desire to listen to someone who had something worth saying, someone whose respect, heroism, and integrity were without equal among national sports icons of his time.

Robinson had something to say because he had been through so much pain and suffering, and so many trials and tribulations, on his way to baseball greatness. He had something to say because he knew so many interesting people, everyone from Dwight Eisenhower and Duke Ellington to Fidel Castro and Ella Fitzgerald. He had something to say because he could give us rare insight into a world unknown to most of us—a lifetime journey from an American nightmare to the American dream. And he had something to say because his passion and compassion were overflowing, often running against the tide of opinions held by other African American leaders of his day.

Jackie Robinson might have had to speak his mind, but like the legions of fans who gathered around the radio in disbelief as he stole another base for the Brooklyn Dodgers, his readers just had to sit up and listen to this truly American pioneer. And, I dare say, it was worth their while. You will know exactly what I mean if you just read ahead and let Robinson share his hard-earned thoughts on baseball and golf, family and friends, civil rights, peace with justice, and politics with principles.

The example Robinson sets through these columns—a passionate life full of righteous anger and bigheartedness—could not be more refreshing than it is in this Age of Athletes Gone Bad, a time when many athletes are notoriously known for shooting one another, abusing drugs and people,

16. There is no written evidence to suggest that Robinson was angered when the NYAN dropped his column. It seems that the column had simply run its course, as many columns do.

or dedicating their lives to consumption upon consumption. If only they, too, would sit up and listen—indeed, if only all of us would pay attention to his words—the legacy that Jackie Robinson had so finely crafted before stealing home plate far too early in the game of life could, and would, make for a world marked by equal justice. At last, what Robinson said of his mentor and friend—"America needs more Mr. Rickeys"[17]—is certainly true of our national icon in this troubling age. The world needs more Jackie Robinsons.

A final word about the columns: I have mentioned that, while Robinson relied on professional writers to help produce his columns, he made sure that the columns clearly, and indisputably, reflected his own voice and beliefs and that he loudly protested when an editor dared to suggest that Robinson's voice had become lost at points in the column. I accept Robinson's judgment on his columns. My own sense is that the columns of Jackie Robinson were—and are—unique insights into his thoughts and feelings about issues ranging from the personal to the political and that it is patently unfair to claim that the columns are somehow less historically valuable than other primary sources (letters, for example) because professional writers assisted him in the process of translating his thoughts onto paper. Robinson stood by his columns—fiercely—as his very own. And it is this important point to recall when we assess their historical value.

17. Letter from Robinson to Branch Rickey, July 24, 1962, Branch Rickey Papers, box 24, folder 14, LOC, Washington, DC.

Beyond
HOME
PLATE

1

On Baseball and Golf

Trouble Ahead—for You, for Me, for My People, and for Baseball

Jackie Robinson broke Major League Baseball's color barrier in August 1945 when he signed a letter of agreement that bound him to the Brooklyn Dodgers. The plan to shatter baseball's color barrier was the brainchild of Branch Rickey, the general manager of the Dodgers. Two months after signing the letter of agreement, Robinson received a formal contract to play for the Montreal Royals, the Dodgers' top farm team, and he made his Major League debut with the Dodgers on April 15, 1947. Throughout his early days in the Major Leagues, Robinson held himself back from "popping off," as he liked to put it, at the fans, players, and managers who taunted him about his race.[1] Rickey had instructed Robinson, for the sake of integrating baseball, to follow the biblical admonition to "turn the other cheek" when facing racist slurs on and off the diamond.[2] Below is Robinson's positive reflection on those early days.

> Source: "Trouble Ahead Needn't Bother You," in *Faith Made Them Champions*, edited by Norman Vincent Peale (Carmel, NY: Guidepost Associates, 1954), 238–41.

I'LL NEVER FORGET THE DAY Branch Rickey, former president of the Brooklyn Dodgers, asked me to join his baseball organization. I would be the first Negro to play in organized baseball—that is, if I were good enough to make the grade.

---

1. See, for instance, *New York Post*, March 30, 1960, 15.
2. See Rampersad, *Jackie Robinson: A Biography*, 127 (see the introduction, n. 3).

Mr. Rickey's office was large and simply furnished. There were four framed pictures on the wall. One was a Kodachrome snapshot of Leo Durocher, the field manager of the Dodgers, and now manager of the New York Giants. Another was a portrait of the late Charlie Barrett, one of the greatest scouts in the game. A third was of General Chennault. And the fourth and largest smiled down on me with calm reassurance, the portrait of the sad, trusting Abraham Lincoln who had pleaded for malice toward none. . . .

This was the never-to-be-forgotten day when our Marines landed on the soil of Japan, August 29, 1945. It was a hot day, with Venetian blinds shutting out the sun, and the Brooklyn clamor of Montague Street mingled with noisy traffic around borough hall.

From behind his desk the big, powerful, bushy-browed Branch Rickey, who seemed a combination of father and boss, mapped out to me his daring strategy to break the color line in major league baseball.

I was excited at the opportunity. It was a tremendous challenge. But was I good enough?

"Mr. Rickey," I said, "it sounds like a dream come true—not only for me but for my race. For seventy years there has been racial exclusion in big league baseball. There will be trouble ahead—for you, for me, for my people, and for baseball."

"Trouble ahead." Rickey rolled the phrase over his lips as though he liked the sound. "You know, Jackie, I was a small boy when I took my first train ride. On the same train was an old couple, also riding for the first time. We were going through the Rocky Mountains. The old man sitting by the window looked forward and said to his wife, 'Trouble ahead, Ma! We're high up over a precipice and we're gonna run right off.'

"To my boyish ears the noise of the wheels repeated 'Trouble-a-head-trouble-ahead. . . .' I never hear train wheels to this day but what I think of this. But our train course bent into a tunnel right after the old man spoke, and we came out on the other side of the mountain. That's the way it is with most trouble ahead in this world, Jackie—if we use the commonsense and courage God gave us. But you've got to study the hazards and build wisely."

I've never forgotten that little story. It helped me through many of the rough moments I was to face in the future. I signed my contract that day with a humble feeling of great responsibility. I prayed that I would be equal to the test.

"God is with us in this, Jackie," Mr. Rickey said quietly. "You know your Bible. It's good simple Christianity for us to face realities and to recognize what we're up against. We can't go out and preach and crusade and bust our heads against a wall. We've got to fight our problems together with tact and commonsense."

To give me experience and seasoning, Mr. Rickey sent me the first year to play with the Montreal Royals, a farm club for the Brooklyn organization. I was the cause of trouble from the start—but we expected it. Preseason exhibition games were canceled because of "mixed athletes," although the official reason was always different.

Some of my teammates may have resented me. If so, I didn't blame them. They had problems enough playing ball without being part of a racial issue. I tried hard not to develop "rabbit ears," a malady picked up by all athletes who are sensitive to abuse and criticism shouted from the fans.

One of my top thrills was my opening game for Montreal at Jersey City. The pressure was on and I was very nervous. But during that contest I slapped out four hits, including a home run. I couldn't have dreamed up a better start.

But as the season began to unroll game after game, my playing grew erratic. I was trying too hard. I knew I had to keep my temper bridled at every turn. Guarding so carefully against outbursts can put a damper on one's competitive spirit.

Every athlete at some time or another likes "to blow his top." It seldom does any harm and acts like a safety valve. A hitter in a slump may drive a ball deep to the infield, then leg it to first, sure that he has beaten the throw. The umpire calls him out. With this the frustrated athlete jerks off his cap, slams it on the ground and thunders all his pent-up irritations at the umpire. The crowd roars its approval or dislike depending on whether the player is on the home or visiting team. The umpire merely turns his back, and the ballplayer, after giving vent to his unhappiness, trots back to the bench feeling much better. It's all a part of the game.

But I didn't dare let loose this way. Many would have dubbed me a "hothead" and pointed to my outburst as a reason why Negroes should not play in organized baseball. This was one of the hardest problems I had to face.

As the season rolled along, however, the players became accustomed to me. My play improved. When the season ended, Montreal had won the Junior World Series. I admit proudly to winning the batting championship of the league with an average of .349.

On April 10, 1947 Branch Rickey made the announcement that gave me my biggest thrill. I was to join the Brooklyn Dodgers and become the first Negro to compete in the major leagues.

It was Montreal all over again, but this time the pressure was much greater, the competition keener, and the stakes tremendous. It wasn't a question so much of a Negro athlete making good as a big leaguer, but whether the whole racial question would be advanced or retarded.

Again I faced the same problems. An opposing player drove a hard grounder to the infield. When he crossed first base his spikes bit painfully into my foot. Accident or deliberate? Who can tell? But the first reaction of a competitive ballplayer is to double up fists and lash out. I saw a blinding red. It took every bit of my discipline to bridle my temper. But when my teammates rushed to my support in white-hot anger, it gave me the warmest feeling I've ever felt. At that moment I belonged.

That year the Dodgers won the pennant. I was thrilled to know that my efforts were considered an important factor in winning. But I also cherished another triumph. Baseball as a whole had come to accept the Negro. Since then a number of Negroes, including Larry Doby, Monte Irvin, Henry Thompson, Willie Mays—and Don Newcomb, Roy Campanella, and Junior Gilliam on the Dodgers—have developed into major league stars. To make the grade they simply had to have the ability. As Mr. Rickey says, a champion is a champion in America, black or white.

Jackie, Sharon, and David Will Have a Real Father

Much to Jackie's disappointment, Branch Rickey sold his ownership in the Dodgers in 1950 and became general manager of the Pittsburgh Pirates. E.

J. "Buzzie" Bavasi later became general manager of the Dodgers, and he and Robinson were never as close as Jackie and Rickey had been.

On December 13, 1956, Bavasi sent Robinson official notice that the team was releasing him; they had traded him to their cross-town rivals, the New York Giants. But Robinson wrecked the deal because by that point, and without telling Dodgers management, he had already signed a contract to begin work as vice president of personnel at Chock Full o' Nuts, a chain of coffee shops based in New York City. To make matters worse, shortly after the Dodgers publicized the trade, an employee of the magazine "Look" leaked an article in which Robinson had announced his retirement from baseball. The magazine had paid Jackie a handsome fee for exclusive rights to publish news about his retirement. The article, reprinted here, and Jackie's decision to retire resulted in a firestorm of criticism from Bavasi and Dodgers owner Walter O'Malley, who had been counting all along on fully effecting his trade to the Giants. As for their part, the Giants management, which must have been baffled, went ahead with the plan for a trade and sent Robinson a contract on January 11, 1957. A few days later Jackie replied that he had decided to be placed on the voluntary retired list. That reply marked the end of a stellar career. In Robinson's ten years with the Dodgers, the team had won six pennants and one World Series.

Leaving his successful baseball career behind, Robinson looked forward to his new life as a businessman with Chock Full o' Nuts. It was a lucrative place for him to land, and Chock's owner, William Black, made it possible for Robinson to continue his demanding volunteer work with the NAACP, especially in his role as national chairman of the NAACP's Freedom Fund Campaign, an effort to increase membership and funds for the civil rights organization.

Source: "Why I'm Quitting Baseball,"
Look, *January 8, 1957, 91–92.*

I'M GLAD I QUIT BASEBALL before I was traded, and I bet I'm not the only one. I'm sure the true Brooklyn fans—the ones I really care about—will be tickled to death that they'll never have to see me playing for another club.

And I'm glad my last season with the Dodgers was a good one and that I had a good Series. Maybe I have another good season or two in me—but at 38, you never know. I'm glad I ended strong.

There are lots of things I'll miss. I love baseball, and I'll miss playing the game. Every inning is a new adventure in baseball. I'll miss that kind of fun. I'll even miss my rhubarbs with the umpires.

I'll miss some of the players I've known, but I'll miss the game more. You play baseball for pleasure and for the money—not to make new friends.

I don't regret any part of the last ten years. There's no reason why I should. Because of baseball, I met a man like Branch Rickey and was given the opportunity to break the major league color line. Because of baseball, I was able to speak on behalf of Negro Americans before the House Un-American Activities Committee and rebuke Paul Robeson for saying most of us Negroes would not fight for our country in a war against Russia. Because of baseball, I made a friend like Marty Stone and got the kind of job I'm stepping into now.

Baseball has been awfully good to me.

There are memories of these ten years I'll cherish all my life: opening day in Jersey City in 1946; the catch I made in 1951 that kept us from losing the pennant that day; the final out in the 1955 Series that made us World Champions; and the time during my first hard year with the Dodgers, when I was standing on first base beside Hank Greenberg of the Pirates. He suddenly turned to me and said, "A lot of people are pulling for you to make good. Don't ever forget that." I never have.

There are a few things I'd like to forget, like the insults from other dugouts that first year, and all the times I blew my top when I shouldn't have. I remember that after being spiked several times at St. Louis, I threatened to do the same to Stan Musial. I've always been sorry for that, because what was going on was not Stan's fault. But most of the irritations of those days I've forgotten. I've never taken my baseball home with me.

Today I'm happier than I've ever been. I know I'll miss the excitement of baseball, but I'm looking forward to new kinds of satisfaction. I'll be able to spend more time with my family. My kids and I will get to know each other better. Jackie and Sharon and David will have a real father they can play with and talk to in the evening and every weekend. They won't have to look for him on TV.

Maybe my sons will want to play ball as I have when they grow up. I'd love it if they do. But I'll see to it that they get a college education first and meet the kind of people who can help them later. That way, they won't have to worry about getting a good job when they quit playing.

Just now, Jackie still feels badly about my quitting the game. It's tough for a ten-year-old to have his dad suddenly turn from a ballplayer into a commuter. I guess it will be quite a change for me too. But someday Jackie will realize that the old man quit baseball just in time.

I Could Not Have Done It Without Mr. Rickey

Robinson considered Branch Rickey to be the father he never had, and Rickey certainly treated Robinson as if he were his own son. When he spoke about Rickey in public, Robinson revealed a side of himself that many individuals simply missed by focusing stereoscopically on his pointed actions in the field of civil rights and politics.

> Source: "Jackie Robinson," New York Post, June 8, 1959, 64.
> Robinson's New York Post column throughout 1959–60 was titled "Jackie Robinson," and the paper used no subtitles for the column to describe its contents further.

TODAY I WANT TO TALK a little about the man who had the greatest influence on my life of anyone outside my family, the man who introduced me to major league baseball—Branch Rickey.

I have always thought and spoken of him as "Mr. Rickey," not because of any formality, nor certainly because of any deference, but just because of the true gentleman that he is. For from the day I first met him in his office in 1945 until the present, I have always been able to count on him for the same kind of support, guidance and just plain friendship that he so warmly gave me in my early years with the Dodger organization.

I well remember the pressures he was subject to in those days back in 1946. The very thought of bringing a Negro player onto a major league team brought responses from some quarters, North and South, not unlike the present day opposition to school desegregation. And for Mr. Rickey, a white man, to take upon himself the initiative to make this step—contrary to the school situation, where Negroes themselves have engineered the fight for equal opportunity—automatically made him a target for particular bitterness, hate and scorn, to those sick whites who considered him a traitor.

This brought about an agonizing concern by his family, for though they shared his conviction that this was the right thing to do, they nonetheless were greatly worried over what he was letting himself in for. He was not well at the time, and they felt the pressures of the so-called Rickey experiment might be too much for his health.

However, Mr. Rickey belittled their fears and focused instead upon his deep sense of obligation—not in any "Messiah" sense, but simply because he felt strongly that racial bars shouldn't exist in our national pastime, and that there was no sense in sitting down and waiting for George to do it. Recognizing wrongs, he felt, implied a personal responsibility to take the initiative in doing whatever one can to correct them.

And so, with the aid of the members of his board, especially George McLaughlin, Mr. Rickey went ahead with his plans. And after a breaking-in period with the Montreal Royals, I was brought onto the Brooklyn squad.

That I was the particular "guinea pig" involved isn't at all important. I believe if Mr. Rickey had thought someone else more suited to the task than I, he would have done what he did nevertheless. But since it was I, then quite naturally I felt a very strong responsibility to make good—for the principle involved, for my fellow Negro Americans, and for Mr. Rickey as well as for myself.

But very frankly, I don't believe I could have done whatever I was able to do without Branch Rickey to advise me. There were times, even in Montreal, when he would call me on the phone to warn me to be on the lookout for trouble, and between the two of us, we were always prepared. I often wondered just how he knew certain incidents were going to happen—his accuracy was little short of uncanny. But as the days passed, I ceased to wonder and merely accepted it without question, for he was always right. . . .

I am proud that through the years, though we are no longer in base-ball together, Branch Rickey and I have maintained the close and warm personal relationship we developed in those early and exciting days. To me, Mr. Rickey is a man blessed with true greatness. For any man who believes in the golden rule and goes to the lengths he did to put it into practice has got to be made of pretty stern stuff.

Throw the Book at the Red Sox

Robinson was not a fan of Tom Yawkey, the owner of the Boston Red Sox, and publicly referred to him as "one of the most bigoted guys in organized baseball."[3] *Under Yawkey's direction, the Red Sox were the last Major League team to integrate. Two months after publication of the following article, however, the team brought up Elijah "Pumpsie" Green from the Minors, and Robinson was delighted enough to praise the decision.*
    Source: New York Post, May 19, 1959, 92.

A FEW WEEKS AGO in Boston, the Massachusetts Commission Against Discrimination held hearings on charges that the Boston Red Sox are guilty of racial discrimination in employment, in violation of state law. Of all the teams in both major leagues, the Red Sox are the only ball club which has never fielded a Negro player.

Truth speaks for itself, and there has never been any question in my mind that the Red Sox management is prejudiced. I can't in the least tell you why, since the Red Sox themselves are the ones hurt mostly by limiting their choice of players on the basis of skin coloring rather than ball-playing. Still, one top Red Sox official has been quoted as having told a Boston newspaperman that the team would use Negro players when the reporter's newspaper began hiring colored employees.

3. "He's No Friend of Tom Yawkey," UPI, September 20, 1967, published in *Quincy (MA) Patriot-Ledger*, September 21, 1967. Filed at Nelson A. Rockefeller Papers Guber-natorial, RG 15, series 34.4, box 42, folder 1129.

I have every confidence that the Massachusetts Commission will do its utmost to eliminate discrimination wherever it occurs. Of course, no one ever has a right to say to any employer, "You must hire this man because he is a Negro, or a Caucasian, or an Oriental," or anything else.

But a growing number of states and cities have passed fair employment legislation which rightly says, "You may not refuse to hire an otherwise qualified person merely on the basis of his race, color or creed. He must be given exactly the same chance as anyone else to earn his livelihood at work for which he can qualify on the basis of ability and training."

In the Red Sox case, I know from experience that a pattern of discrimination has long been established. Back in 1945, Sam Jethroe, Marvin Williams and I were brought to Boston by Wendell Smith for a tryout by the Red Sox. We were taken to Fenway Park, and there for most of a day we were given free rein to put on a display for the Red Sox brass.

It was one of these days when it seemed as if nothing could go wrong. We hit, we fielded, we made double plays. Yet, it was no surprise whatsoever that none of us was ever invited to join the Red Sox team. We were given a *full* tryout. But under the circumstances, I can't honestly say it was a *fair* one.

Personally, I'm very happy that soon afterwards Branch Rickey signed me for the Brooklyn Dodgers, for this to me was the greatest ball club of them all. But in the thirteen years since, despite the breakdown of the color bar by every other team in the major leagues, Boston has not yet been able to "find" a good Negro player, as one Red Sox spokesman told the Commission hearing.

. . . The Red Sox can make excuses and charge "agitation" by the NAACP or me or anyone else. The fact remains that if they were really interested in proving they are not biased, they could easily do so by changing their hiring policies.

Recently they gave another tryout, this time to Elijah "Pumpsie" Green. Green was taken along for spring training in Arizona, where he lived away from the rest of the team. And again it was no surprise that when the Red Sox came East to begin the season, Pumpsie Green was sent to a farm club—where, incidentally, he has turned out to be an outstanding player.

. . . But Green himself is not the point. Neither were Sam Jethroe, Marvin Williams, Charlie Neal, Jackie Robinson, nor any of the others they had chances to hire, and didn't.

The rub lies in the consistent pattern of refusal. It is the Red Sox themselves who are not "ready" to judge a ballplayer by his ability rather than his skin. And if this is the fact in the case of Pumpsie Green—as I suspect it is—then I hope the commission throws the book at them.

Americans can no longer afford—nor should they tolerate—either a lynching in the South or a "gentleman's agreement" in the North. Both are cut from the same ugly cloth. And both must be stamped out wherever they occur.

Out of the Dugout Charged Ralph Branca

Robinson enjoyed long-term friendships with baseball players he deeply respected, including Ralph Branca, the Brooklyn Dodgers pitcher who became infamous for giving up a home run to Bobby Thomson in the ninth inning of the 1951 playoff game against the New York Giants. The "shot heard 'round the world" propelled the Giants into the pennant race, leaving Dodgers fans deflated yet again. The column here gives a peek at the discrimination that Robinson suffered, as well as the support he enjoyed, when he joined the Dodgers in 1947. Although Robinson notes the resistance of St. Louis fans, he might have drawn attention as well to the Philadelphia fans. Their resistance to Robinson was among the worst in Major League Baseball, particularly when they threw a black cat onto the field during a game with the Dodgers.
Source: New York Post, May 22, 1959, 96.

SPRING TO ME—now that I'm no longer a baseball player—means not only following the teams and checking the box scores. It also means getting out and actively involving myself in my second sports love: golf. But even while tramping up and down the golf course following that little white ball, it's difficult to stay away from thoughts of the baseball diamond. And especially if you're shooting 18 holes with former Dodger pitching ace Ralph Branca.

Just last week, Ralph and I joined a couple of friends for an outing. Playing golf with Ralph brought back to me thoughts of the wonderful days we had as teammates, and particularly of one of the many things he did to help out the so-called "Rickey Experiment."

The year was 1947. The Dodgers were playing a crucial series with the Cardinals in St. Louis, Mo. I say "crucial" not only because of the relative league standings of the two teams involved. It was crucial also because St. Louis, a Southern town, was the seat of some hardback resistance to the idea of introducing a Negro player into major league baseball.

St. Louis had been the source of many rumors that the Dodgers had a ball club that was greatly disturbed internally over Branch Rickey's insistence—despite the open objections of some of the players—in buying up my contract from Montreal and bringing me into the Brooklyn team. There were many fans, not only in St. Louis, who doubted there could be any harmony on such a team as ours, and were just waiting for evidence of a split in order to crow, "I told you so!"

It was a very close ball game. Nippy Jones of the Cards had been giving us more trouble with his bat than even Stan Musial, and I think all baseball fans know how well Stan could hit the Dodger pitching.

Nippy popped a ball up and I, playing first base at the time, thought only of catching it and getting Nippy out. I ran as fast as I could with my eye glued to the ball, momentarily forgetting that it would be impossible to stop before crashing into the concrete stands or the Brooklyn dugout. But on I ran, made the catch, and then within that split second realized that I was in trouble. I couldn't stop!

But, suddenly, out of the dugout charged Ralph Branca. And in front of the thousands of St. Louis fans—many of whom were wondering about the relationships on our team—he caught me in his arms, keeping me from certain injury.

Ralph told me later his only thought was of preventing me from getting hurt, and keeping the team intact. But I know from my many subsequent experiences with Branca that also, perhaps without even thinking about it, he was glad of the chance to prove the St. Louis rumors unfounded, by demonstrating his human concern for a fellow teammate, no matter what his color. . . .

It was good to meet with Ralph and shoot a game of golf on a lovely spring day. And it's good also to reminisce a bit about our playing days together.

Call it spring fever . . . or something.

Willie Mays—and Too Many Negroes on the Giants?

Civic leaders welcomed Willie Mays with open arms when he arrived in San Francisco to play for the Giants following the 1957 season, but the star ballplayer faced strong resistance from city residents while trying to purchase a house in a white neighborhood. After city officials intervened and Mays bought the house, someone shattered one of his windows with a bottle containing a threatening note. In the following column on Mays, Robinson refers to Giants owner Horace Stoneham, manager Bill Rigney, and director of operations Charles "Chub" Feeney.
Source: New York Post, August 17, 1959, 48.

. . . STILL, whenever you have a Willie Mays on your team, you can't help but have a club to be reckoned with. It's been hard for me to understand, though, if 'Frisco is really a fine baseball town, how on earth they haven't taken Willie Mays more to heart. If what we hear is correct, then off the field, Mays has been having a pretty rough time. I'm sure that Willie, being the great major leaguer he is, will continue to hustle and try for the big play regardless of what anyone does or says, but it's more than unfortunate that he hasn't obtained the popularity and appreciation his great play would seem to merit.

I've said many times before, and I don't mind repeating, that in my opinion Willie Mays can—and probably will—be as great a baseball player as ever trotted onto a diamond. The only thing that could possibly prevent it is Willie himself. It may sometimes be hard, but he must not allow anything or anyone to distract him from doing the tremendous day-to-day job he is capable of. For without distraction, Willie's natural talents and great love for the game could carry him straight to the pinnacle of baseball greatness. . . .

I was greatly surprised and concerned when it came to my attention the other day that there's been grumbling in some baseball circles that the Giants have too many Negroes on the team. Of course, I've been through all this before. When I broke into baseball, even one Negro was far too many to a lot of people. Later, when the Dodgers sometimes played five Negro players at a time—as has happened in San Francisco lately—there were crude jokes cracked and snide caricatures printed in some quarters, North and South.

But just as the Dodgers management ignored this pettiness of a sick minority, I have every confidence that Giants owner Horace Stoneham and his staff will also. There have always been people who would rather keep their prejudices and lose than to accept assistance from a different-colored hand than their own. But if anybody thinks the Giants are going to be pressured into refusing to play the best man for each job, no matter what his race, religion, or creed, then I don't think they know Horace Stoneham, Chub Feeney or Bill Rigney very well. It is obvious the Giants and their fans are interested in one objective only: winning ball games. It is also obvious that those who grumble for a return to bias in baseball have picked themselves a lost cause.

How to Be a Good Loser

Although this column addresses the role of parenting and Little League baseball, it also offers an indirect glimpse into Robinson's life philosophy— one that extols the "will to win" in a competitive society while also making room for those individuals who lose the competition. Robinson was a fierce competitor in sports, civil rights, and politics, and he often wielded his competitive spirit on behalf of those who lacked power and influence in society.
Source: New York Post, August 21, 1959, 48.

. . . [L]IKE ANYTHING ELSE, it has its pros and cons. But despite the harsh cries of some detractors, and despite some very real problems which do exist, there is no doubt in my mind whatsoever that Little League base-ball is of great benefit to our kids, and to our community.

I well recall during the first year how upset our youngsters became when they lost a game. Today, they are still bothered by defeat, but now there is greater realization by both the kids and their parents that one of the two teams has to lose and that the world hasn't come to an end if the home team hasn't slaughtered the opposition.

Of course, winning is the great American way, and all our modern fairytale movies and success stories give rise to the assumption that anything Junior decides to do will inevitably be a howling success. And undoubtedly we must instill in our youngsters a will to win, since this is the prime basis of all competition. Still, we do them—and ourselves—a great disservice if we don't also develop an understanding of what it is to lose. For how to be a good loser is perhaps one of the most important lessons of life, and if carefully learned at Little League age, then adjustment to the natural give-and-take of later years can be a lot easier.

On an individual as well as a team level, our coaches in Stamford have, I think, been very patient with the players in teaching them that no one can expect to hit the game-winning homerun every time he comes to bat. They work with these kids pointing out their mistakes and showing them how to correct them, and show remarkable restraint in keeping their criticisms on a positive level. The attitudes of Little League officials are also of great importance, and I think we've been fortunate in having good ones.

When it comes to another vital aspect of the Little League picture, however, there seems to me to be room for a great deal of improvement. And that is in the attitudes of some of our parents. Very often, after Junior has been patiently taught a healthy competitive outlook which takes winning and losing in reasonable stride, a parent will undo much of the good work that has been done by his own selfish outlook.

I've heard parents put pressure on their youngsters by threatening to deprive them of some privilege if they don't get that base hit, or dangling lavish rewards if they do. Sometimes they berate their youngster in the presence of others when he hasn't done well, or over-inflate his ego when he has. And when this happens, I can just see the hours of patient effort going down the drain. In fact, sometimes I think if we had coaches and officials to work with the parents, the kids would take care of themselves.

Once, my wife Rachel arrived at one of our Little League games while it was in progress, and the mother of one of the players called out to her that our son, Jack, had struck out. My wife smiled, and answered, "Well, it won't be the last time, so it's not important." But the mother indignantly retorted:

"Oh, but it is important. *My* son was on first base!"

I'm quite convinced that Little League baseball can be of great value to our youngsters if only our adults give them half a chance.

Another *Amos-n-Andy* Cartoon of Negro Players

A radio show that began in 1928, "Amos-n-Andy" featured white actors depicting African American friends as bumbling, illiterate, and inarticulate—and thus hilarious to many white Americans fond of minstrel shows. When it later appeared on television, the show featured black actors, but the demeaning stereotypes continued. African American leaders, especially in the media and the NAACP, had long protested the show as racially demeaning, and in the column here Robinson appeals to "Amos-n-Andy" with this history of protest in mind.

The column, which offers a blistering critique of an article on the private lives of black ballplayers, is especially fascinating in the sense that it brings to the surface some of the lingering tensions between Robinson and the white sporting press. Like other African American players who played a pioneering role in baseball, Robinson was very wary of sportswriters who seemed more interested in their private lives than in the racial injustices they suffered as blacks. And, as the column below suggests, Jackie was especially concerned about articles that seemed to fuel negative stereotypes about black men. Robinson no doubt felt that some key members of the sporting press were just as racist in their reporting as were some of the players and coaches whom pioneering black players had to endure on the playing field.

One other significant point to note here is that in the following column Robinson does not comment at all on a significant part of the article he criticizes—namely, its attention to the tensions in relations between African American and Hispanic players. Unfortunately, then, Robinson does not

offer any answer to the question of whether the Latinization of professional
baseball posed any concerns to him at this point in his life, as it apparently
did to other black players.

Source: *New York Post,* March 23, 1960, 88.

I'VE JUST READ AN ARTICLE in the current issue of *Sports Illustrated*
magazine entitled "The Private World of the Negro Ballplayer." And with
all due respect to fellow *Post* columnist Murray Kempton, I don't at all
agree with him that this piece, by Robert Boyle, should be classified among
"the body of satisfactory literature by white men about Negroes." In many
respects I found this article unbelievable, insulting and degrading, both to
Negro ballplayers and to the intelligence of *Sports Illustrated*'s readers.

Though some of Boyle's long treatise is written with understanding
and appreciation for the unique position Negroes occupy in major league
baseball, much of it seems to be a deliberate picking-out of minor details
he thinks will make for offbeat reading. In the process he largely makes
these players seem to be a bunch of purposely clannish, ignorant and secre-
tive players who refuse to go along with progress. If Boyle really thinks he
has managed to enter and understand what he calls the "private world" of
the Negro ballplayer, I submit he is sadly mistaken. For his article comes
through to me as just another Amos 'n Andy cartoon of what many whites
think Negroes are like.

Boyle proclaims his discovery that Negro players have a secret code of
their own. Apparently having broken this code he goes on to list as examples such items as: a Negro player does not criticize another Negro player
in front of a white; Negro players do not fight each other; they refuse to go
out socially with white players; they hold conversations in code in front of
whites so the whites won't know what they are talking about; and a Negro
player does not mention a girl by name to another Negro player because—
and here he quotes Willie Mays—"the other guy may be going out with
the girl, too."

In my ten years in the major leagues I found that ballplayers—Negro
or white—are always on guard about talking to members of the press. They
have to be, to protect their jobs as well as their reputations. Why Boyle
thinks these players would trust him to the point of being open and frank

with him about their private affairs, I don't know. At the very best, these are generalizations Boyle formulated himself from isolated scraps of information. For if there ever existed any such code—secret or otherwise—I never heard about it when I played baseball.

I particularly resent the comment he attributes to Willie Mays. Knowing Mays as I do, I seriously doubt that this is what he actually said—but if he did, then I'm greatly disappointed in him. Negro women have often been maligned and degraded by those who seek to picture them as traditionally loose in moral character. This lie has been allowed to flourish for far too long. And though there are Negro camp-followers (as well as white), it seems to me greatly insulting to imply that this is the circle of companionship that Negro ballplayers confine themselves to.

It took a long time to obtain democracy in America's best-loved sport. Today Negro players are well integrated into the game, and though there still are problems, by and large they are accepted as individual players whose personalities, interests and abilities vary just as much as they do among their white fellow teammates. Any attempt to lump them all together and label them "different" on racial grounds is a disservice to them and to the sport, as well as at variance with the facts.

O'Malley Couldn't Get Along with Anyone Who Appreciated Rickey

In this column about Dodgers owner Walter O'Malley, Robinson cites a section of his forthcoming book, "Wait Till Next Year," which describes a meeting between him, Rachel, and O'Malley. According to Robinson's recollection of the meeting, he and Rachel disputed O'Malley's criticism that Robinson was a prima donna, extolled the personal concern and loyalty that Branch Rickey had always shown them, and complained that hotel arrangements on the road did not allow for the Robinson children to sleep in a room adjoining their own. Robinson refers below to Buzzie Bavasi, who directed baseball operations for the Dodgers, and to Fresco Thompson, who oversaw the Dodgers' farm teams.

Source: New York Post, May 13, 1960, 96.

WALTER O'MALLEY is the subject of an article in the current issue of the *Saturday Evening Post*. Among other things, writer Marvin Durslag reports the Dodger president as having some pretty definite things to say about a former Dodger ballplayer named Jackie Robinson. . . . I find it exceedingly hard to believe O'Malley could have said some of the things Durslag has written.

The article quotes O'Malley as saying: "When I took over the presidency of the club, Jackie and I had a talk. I said, 'Jackie, if you've been under any wraps at all, about turning the other cheek and all that, I would feel better just thinking of you as a ballplayer who is doing the best for your team. If you feel that a situation calls for you to lose your temper, you've got to lose it, I guess.'"

I suggest to the writer that if he really wants to know what happened at the one meeting I ever had with O'Malley that he read pages 256–262 of my new book with Carl Rowan, *Wait Till Next Year*, which will be out the week after next. For the version in Durslag's article couldn't be further from the truth.

In the *Post* article O'Malley—if quoted correctly—says he thought he and Robinson "got along pretty well." The fact is, O'Malley couldn't get along with anyone who appreciated Branch Rickey and I am Rickey fan no. 1. O'Malley's great sensitivity to Mr. Rickey is self-evident in another quotation:

"After we beat the White Sox in the [1959] World Series, I received a telegram from Rickey in which I'm sure he meant for me to read between the lines. It stated, 'Congratulations to you, Buzzie and Fresco on the great victory of your team.'"

Why O'Malley feels he must interpret this as anything other than a straightforward message of congratulations is beyond me. Or does he really resent having vice presidents Bavasi and Thompson share in the credit . . . ? This is typical of O'Malley, however, and anyone who has ever had dealings with him will look at this and laugh. I'm sure the N.Y. City government could testify, after their dealings with him, that if it's good for O'Malley, you can get along with him, but if you differ, you're in trouble.

Durslag also quotes O'Malley as stating, "Jackie has a purpose in life," namely, being an "expert" in the field of publicity, and that I know "a great way to attract attention is to get the Dodgers involved somehow."

I might point out both to Durslag—who seems to feel my criticisms are too "loud"—and to O'Malley that I neither asked to be discussed in their article, nor was my permission sought. If either gentleman thinks I've received too much attention, then I suggest they could easily have avoided adding to it by leaving me out of their discussion.

It is important to note that the anger that bursts forth in this column was not always present when Robinson wrote about O'Malley. In a May 12, 1959, article, for instance, he praised the Dodgers owner for giving Roy Campanella financial and emotional support following the car accident that left the famous catcher partially paralyzed.

Consider Abilities, Not Color, When Hiring Manager

When Robinson shattered the color barrier in 1947, Bill Veeck owned the Cleveland Indians. And by the time Robinson wrote the following column, Veeck had become part-owner of the Chicago White Sox. From Robinson's perspective, no one in professional baseball, including Bill Veeck, could come close to equaling the quality of legacy created by Branch Rickey.
Source: New York Post, September 2, 1960, 60.

BILL VEECK is a man who has often been ranked along with Branch Rickey as one of the most liberal and progressive men in baseball. Shortly after Mr. Rickey and I began our "great experiment" in 1947, Veeck followed suit by signing Larry Doby to the Cleveland Indian roster as the first Negro in the American League. And ever since he has given every indication that ability, not color, is his criterion for evaluating ballplayers and other people as well.

But I must confess being greatly surprised and disappointed in some of what Veeck has to say in an article—written with Louie Robinson in the August issue of *Ebony* Magazine—entitled "Are There Too Many Negroes in Baseball?"

Happily, Veeck quickly dismisses that question in the article. Pointing out that the question assumes there is "a sufficient number of prejudiced people who don't necessarily want to see a preponderance of any race or color not their own," he goes on to say he doesn't think this has been a factor so far. "I know that the White Sox would put the best possible team on the field if all the players were pink with blue dots," Veeck continues, "because in the final analysis it is important for us to try to win." On this basis, he adds, "there could hardly ever be too many Negroes in baseball."

But then Veeck turns to the question of a Negro manager in the major leagues and there his courage seems to fail him a little. Though he concedes the time is probably not too far off when there will be a Negro manager, Bill, nevertheless, finds it necessary to set different standards of "acceptance" for a Negro in this job than for whites. Writes Veeck:

"Of course a man will have to have more stability to be a Negro coach or manager and slower to anger than if he were white. This sounds unfair, but it is, nevertheless, a statement of fact, because he will be a target, just as Jackie Robinson was as the first player. The first Negro manager will have his own club to contend with (although this won't be too much of a problem, since players will respect baseball sagacity) in addition to the fans, who will be quicker to jump on him for any mistakes that might occur."

Veeck then adds: "I think Jackie Robinson could have made a good manager, but I'm not sure that his temperament would be that of a basically successful major league manager."

First of all, I think I've made it abundantly clear that Jackie Robinson is not at all interested in returning to baseball in any capacity. I enjoyed my 10 years as a player in the big leagues and—had the opportunity presented itself when I left—I might have considered becoming a manager. But it did not and now I'm so satisfied with my present work that I can't conceive of any offer which could tempt me enough to become a baseball manager. So the question of my qualifications or "temperament" as a manager isn't at all important.

What is important, however, is the fact that a man like Bill Veeck should find it necessary to retreat from the hard-won standard in baseball today that a man's abilities are what count, not his color or his "temperament," when it comes to considering a man for management responsibility. I'd hate to think that a Leo Durocher, a Casey Stengel—or even a Bill Veeck, were he interested—would find themselves barred from becoming managers if they were Negro instead of white. None of these gentlemen could be accused of lack of "temperament" and none could prove a "particularly subdued personality"—which is the term Veeck used in a letter to me defending his views.

I think Negro Americans have long since proved their right to be considered on exactly the same basis as anyone else in baseball—as if any race should ever have to "prove" itself to anybody. Why it should now become a different matter in terms of management qualifications is unworthy of the reputation of a Bill Veeck, as well as offensive to the very core of a great American sport. . . .

I Won't Crawl to the Hall of Fame

Robinson explains the importance of principles over politics in relation to the pending 1962 elections to the Baseball Hall of Fame. It was his first year of eligibility for election, and there is no doubt that he hoped to capture enough ballots to gain entry into the Hall.

> Source: "I Won't Crawl to the Hall of Fame," *New York Amsterdam News*, January 12, 1962, 1, 11. Beginning January 20, 1962, "Home Plate" became the main title of Robinson's columns with the *New York Amsterdam News*. The titles listed in following *Amsterdam News* columns are subtitles that appeared under the title "Home Plate."

THE MAIL has been unusually heavy and the telephone calls numerous. The sports writers of America are now in the process of balloting on nominees for baseball's Hall of Fame. People have been calling and writing because, for the first time, the name of a Negro—Jackie Robinson—has been placed in nomination.

The fact that my name has come up for consideration has given rise to printed conjecture about how I will fare in the voting due to the charge that my "fiery temper" made me a "much hated player."

I am not going to pretend that I wouldn't be thrilled to be elected to the Hall of Fame. I believe that every man who ever got into a baseball uniform recognizes that election to the Hall of Fame is the ultimate, the Academy Award of the sport.

On the other hand, I'd like to make it perfectly clear that I do not think I deserve election simply because I was the first Negro in baseball. I do not feel I deserve rejection either, simply because I directed my "fiery temper" against violations of my personal dignity and civil rights and the civil rights of the people for whom I have such deep concern.

There are standards and requisites clearly defined for election to the Hall of Fame. I believe they include playing ability, sportsmanship, character, contribution to your team and to baseball in general. If, in the honest opinion of the sportswriters of America, I qualify in accordance with these requisites, then I will feel genuinely happy about it. If I honestly qualify and if I am refused the honor because I fought and argued for the principles in which I believe, so be it. Were it possible to make a swap between violating my convictions and winning this high mark of baseball immortality, I would unquestioningly select adherence to my principles and my integrity.

I left baseball because my integrity was challenged by one executive in the game. I have always been vigilant to keep that integrity intact. So I left with no regrets. I maintained and I still cherish the feeling that I can get up in the morning and look myself square in the face in the mirror of my own conscience.

Does this mean I believe I was always one hundred percent right in my squawks and in hassles in which I became involved?

I am not so stupid or arrogant as to feel that way.

I made mistakes at times and I apologized for them as fast as I recognized they were mistakes. There is one mistake I tried never to make—and that was to sell myself or my beliefs for money, for friendship, for approval or for awards and honors.

I have stated above that I would not consider myself qualified for election to the Hall of Fame based simply on the fact that I was the first Negro in baseball. I must say in all honesty, however, that looking at baseball today and what has happened in the game, I do not believe that the pioneer role can be completely overlooked. Whether the honors for this belong to Branch Rickey or to me—or to both of us—it is an incontrovertible fact that the breakthrough in America's favorite sport was the beginning of a more democratic image for that sport and for America.

Needless to say, it was also healthy for the box office. . . .

Let the chips fall where they may. Let the best man win.

I do not wish to sound indifferent. I am not indifferent. I am indifferent only to those who condemn me because I prefer to be true to myself.

My son Jackie will be awfully proud if his father becomes a member of the Hall of Fame. But he won't cry if this doesn't happen—as he cried when I left the game. He won't cry because I think he knows his old man would rather go down in his son's memory as a guy who played it straight from the shoulder and from his beliefs than to become a member of a thousand Halls of Fame.

Robinson was elected, and Richard Nixon took the occasion to pen a letter to the new Hall of Famer. "And I can truly say," Nixon wrote, "that never was an honor more richly deserved and that no man could enter the Hall of Fame with better credentials."[4]

The Hall of Fame Awaits You

In this column, Robinson takes stock of his life after winning election to the Baseball Hall of Fame and reflects on what baseball has meant to him. The column offers a striking contrast to some of the statements Robinson made shortly after his retirement. At that point, having suffered through a public relations battle with the Dodgers about their intent to trade him to the Giants, Robinson occasionally appeared to be a bitter man with little concern for baseball. But his love of the game endured, and Rachel Robinson has described her husband as a true fan who could not sit still while watching a televised game.

Source: New York Amsterdam News, February 3, 1962, 9.

4. Letter from Richard Nixon to Robinson, January 29, 1962, Jackie Robinson Papers (JRP), box 5, folder 11.

LAST WEEK, before the announcement that the Baseball Writers Association of America had elected me to the Hall of Fame, I had been positive that I would not achieve this singular honor at this time.

Now that I have been elected, I want one thing to be known. I consider this honor the greatest which could have come to me. Furthermore, I want to do two things. I want to prove that I really belong and I want to use this wonderful opportunity, if I possibly can, to help unfortunate kids who are struggling for a break in life.

When I look back over my life—back to seventeen or eighteen years ago—I can remember times when I didn't know how I was going to get my next meal. I made up my mind a long time ago that this would have to change and the only way I could change it was by making something of myself.

I feel so strongly and deeply about being a member of the Hall of Fame that I am almost at a loss to explain those feelings to readers of this column. I just want to say that if this can happen to a guy whose parents were virtually slaves, a guy from a broken home, a guy whose mother worked as a domestic from sunup to sundown for a number of years; if this can happen to someone who, in his early years, was a delinquent and who learned that he had to change his life—then it can happen to you kids out there who think that life is against you.

I mean this for all kids—not just youngsters of my race—but all. I make no apology for being particularly interested in the youngsters of my own race, for they belong to a minority which has been abused and held back for many years. To them I say that I find so much inspiration in what has happened to me. It points up and proves that there are a lot of wonderful people of other races who believe in us enough and believe in real democracy enough to stand up and be counted when it counts to be counted.

It is especially significant to me that I have had serious differences with a number of the men who belong to the distinguished groups which elected me.

These men elected me in spite of the fact that they knew and know now that Jackie Robinson would always say and do only the things in which he believed.

In doing so, they refuted what was once told me by one of their own craft—an excellent newspaperman. This writer told me that I had lost and would lose many honors and awards if I continued to express myself exactly the way I felt.

I know that I have missed honors and awards because of this in the past. This—the greatest honor of them all—means so much to me because I have received it and remained true to my own convictions. I would give it up gladly if I had to in order to keep my self-respect. However, it feels pretty wonderful having both.

I have accepted election to the Hall as a challenge—and as I said before, it will remind me always how tremendously fortunate I have been, how wonderful people have been to me.

All this means that I must constantly prove I deserve what I have received by trying to do all in my power to help others.

Shortly after visiting Cooperstown for his induction, Robinson accepted Rachel's advice that he seek a meeting with O'Malley to discuss their strained relationship. Although the meeting never happened, O'Malley cooperated in making Jackie Robinson Day a success at Dodger Stadium on June 16, 1965, and the two men exchanged pleasant letters following the event.

Pee Wee Reese
Man of Courage

Pee Wee Reese played shortstop for the Dodgers (1940–42, 1946–57), and he and Robinson turned more than a few dazzling double plays during their tenure together. More important, though, was Robinson's deep, and long-lasting, appreciation of Reese, whose family roots were in the segregated South, for standing by him in the early, and enormously difficult, years of fighting blatant racism in Major League Baseball.
Source: New York Amsterdam News, July 7, 1962, 11.

A FEW DAYS AGO, from Louisville, Kentucky, it was announced that Pee Wee Reese, the former Brooklyn Dodger captain, had quit under fire as a candidate for membership on the Citizens Human Rights Commission. According to newspaper reports, Reese was criticized by a mixed group of citizens because he operates—or has a connection with—a bowling alley which bars Negroes.

As firmly as this writer is opposed to any and all forms of segregation, this news disturbs me deeply. For, in my book, Pee Wee Reese is and has been a decent, courageous guy who knew how to stand up and speak out on the race issue where and when it counted.

Very few people know as well as I do the kind of courage of which Pee Wee Reese is capable. I can safely say that one of the great contributions to my own personal fight to integrate major league baseball was made by Reese. Of his own will, Reese chose to become my partner during the trying experiences of those early days.

I shall never forget an incident in Boston at the very beginning of my major league career. It is difficult these days, when there are Negroes in virtually all the lineups, to realize how bitter the opposition was against a Negro ballplayer—opposition on the part of the public, the front offices of the ball clubs and the players themselves.

In Boston, during a game, there were some players on the bench of the opposing team who had heard how Pew Wee had accepted me as a teammate and friend. They knew that he had played golf with me and Wendell Smith of the *Pittsburgh Courier* on a golf course where people were probably shocked to see Negroes. These players decided to heckle Reese about being a white Southerner willing to fraternize with a Negro.

One of them called out a sneering demand whether Reese and I were going to have dinner together after the game. Another shouted jeeringly that Reese's "grandpappy" would cut off his mint julep when he learned his grandson was socializing with a Negro.

Pee Wee ignored the riding for a while. Then, as the bench jockeys really got loud, he did a simple and significant thing. He walked over to me and put his arm around my shoulder. We talked for a minute. Neither one of us, to this day, remembers what we were talking about. We do know what we were saying to the agitators and to the world.

We were saying that we were teammates—white man from the South and Negro from California by way of Georgia. We were saying we were there to play ball and to beat hell out of the Boston team. We were saying that all the sneers meant nothing.

Pee Wee didn't only show this kind of courage in public. He and I have spent hours discussing the kind of problems he faced when he was a youngster in the South, observing the prejudiced attitudes of family and friends. He has told me this caused conflicts in him because he never could feel that a man should be judged merely by the color of his skin.

I am not defending Pee Wee Reese if he is guilty of discrimination against Negroes who want to use his bowling alley. I am saying simply that I hope a tragic mistake hasn't been made and an injustice done against a guy whom I have found to be 100 percent in the past.

We keep hollering for one world—and for integration and racial justice. And we should. But we must learn that we have to give out as well as receive. We must give friendship and understanding if we are to get friendship and understanding in return. And we have got to give it, not only to each other, but also to our white brothers who have demonstrated their willingness to stand up and be counted when the racist chips are down.

In "The Boys of Summer," his famous book on the Brooklyn Dodgers, Roger Kahn wrote about Reese's reaction to the charges leveled against him: "'Look,' Reese said. 'What happened was that a black team wanted to use it on a night when all the alleys were taken by a league. Now maybe that league was all-white. I don't check on all the customers. In this climate, charges get wild. But hell'—disgust sounded—'I wouldn't run a segregated anything.'"[5]

A Baseball Education

A little more than twenty years before Robinson authored this column, the NAACP had protested the American Red Cross's refusal to accept blood plasma from African Americans. On December 30, 1941, Walter White,

5. Roger Kahn, *The Boys of Summer*, excerpted in Andrew Paul Mele, *A Brooklyn Dodgers Reader* (Jefferson, NC: McFarland, 2005), 212.

the executive secretary of the NAACP, even made a direct plea to the US secretary of war, arguing (to no avail) that the blood plasma of blacks was no different from the plasma of whites. The segregation of blood in the early part of the twentieth century was practiced not just in Louisiana (which Robinson writes of here) but also throughout the country. Clearly visible in the column below is Robinson's special interest in protecting children from the ravages wrought by racist adults. Nothing angered him more than seeing innocent children suffer indignities perpetrated by racist adults.

Source: New York Amsterdam News, January 26, 1963, 4.

I READ SEVERAL YEARS AGO that a six-year-old white boy in Louisiana died for want of blood plasma. This is a country noted for the humanitarian gift of lifeblood—both on the battlefield in defense of noble ideas and in everyday life to combat critical disease.

Yet this small boy's life was in jeopardy and the great blood banks of the American Red Cross could not be used to help him for, in Louisiana, there is a law that "white" and "Negro blood" must not flow together— even in lifesaving blood banks.

I wonder how easy it would be to convince the parents of this dying boy, no matter how deep their beliefs on racial issues, that their son's agony was necessary to perpetuate the great stone of segregation. I wonder how impressed they would be, as their youngster gasped for breath, by the argument that all our racial questions will be settled by long, drawn-out "education."

It is inconceivable to me how any of our fellow countrymen can preach the doctrine of "patience" and "education" in these days as a substitute for forthright action to implement all the handmade and God-made laws regarding the brotherhood of humans and the fatherhood of the Maker.

If the argument that we must wait for "education" had been applied in organized baseball, it would have been centuries before this great American sport became truly democratic. The true "education" which we received in organized baseball came about through the opportunity of sharing a relationship, colored boys with white boys, with getting to know each other.

Don't you remember all the talk about the problems which would arise if someone tried to allow white and colored players to play, work and travel together, to use the same shower and share the same hotels? Of course! The problems did arise and they were dealt with beautifully. We got an education.

This is why I believe those who preach delay are wrong. This kind of "education," they advocate, is taking its terrible toll in human dignity and the kind of situation which condemns a six-year-old white boy to death for want of blood. . . .

If America Followed Baseball's Example

Lying behind this column was Robinson's deeply held belief that his African American colleagues in baseball had an obligation to speak out about racial injustice and take visible action to destroy it. In the past Jackie had felt keen disappointment when some black players—for example, Maury Wills (Dodgers), Roy Campanella (Dodgers), and Willie Mays (Giants)—were not as vocal or militant as he thought they should have been.

Robinson had found Campanella to be especially reactionary on civil rights issues during their time together on the Brooklyn Dodgers. But in the column here, Robinson extols his former fellow player, largely paralyzed after a car accident, for making an unqualified public stance against segregation in an essay he contributed to Robinson's new book, "Baseball Has Done It." Robinson refers below to Bobby Bragan, the Dodgers catcher who initially opposed Robinson's presence on the team in 1947; Larry Doby, an African American player signed by the Cleveland Indians shortly after Robinson made his debut with the Dodgers; and Dodgers pitching ace Carl Erskine.

Source: New York Amsterdam News, May 30, 1964, 23.

I HAVE JUST FINISHED writing notes of gratitude to some of the top crop of players in baseball who were kind enough to become contributors to my new book, *Baseball Has Done It*, published by J. P. Lippincott Company. . . .

My disappointment that Maury Wills and Willie Mays were not willing to participate in this book was more than balanced by my delight at the uncompromising stand taken by Campy, my former teammate who hit hard at the immoral and unjust practices of discrimination and segregation.

Campy is so well-loved and respected by so many people that his involvement in the civil rights cause will mean a tremendous plus to that cause.

There are some significant and poignant words in this book. Birmingham-born Bobby Bragan writes: "Baseball has accepted Negroes. No resentment stems from Southerners in baseball anymore. When a Negro puts a run up on the scoreboard, no one questions the color of the run."

Larry Doby confides: "My Southern teammates were more reliable than some Northerners. I knew where I stood with them. After they knew me better, they were regular guys on the field. A Northerner might give you the glad hand, but after he discovers that you have as much ability as he, he's a different person altogether."

Carl Erskine admits: "When you're on a club with a Negro, you know the guy is flesh and blood, and eats and sleeps, and rides a train with you, and sweats with you out there on the field, and he helps your club more than anybody else, and then you walk into a restaurant and they say everybody can eat but him, then you really understand what it's like to be a Negro."

Campy weighs in with: "It's a horrible thing to sit here and realize what a situation like this means to an individual—to be born an American and have to go to court to find out how much of an American he is.

"It's a horrible thing to be born in this country and go along with all the rules, laws and regulations and have to battle in court for the right to go to the movies—to wonder which store my children can go into in the South to try on a pair of shoes or where to sleep in a hotel.

"I am a Negro and I am part of this. I don't care what anyone says about me. I feel it as deep as anyone, and so do my children."

Yes, baseball has blazed the trail for America. If America followed baseball's example, we'd have a finer country and a stronger position in the world. . . .

No Negro Managers?
Go Out and Get Some!

While he was still playing ball, Robinson sat for an interview that was pub-
lished under the title "Why Can't I Manage in the Majors?" In the inter-
view, Robinson recounted that his friends approached him with all kinds of
advice, positive and negative, after they had read that he was being consid-
ered for a managing position in the Pacific Coast League. Here is the way
Robinson remembered the event:

Almost immediately I began hearing from friends by mail, phone and
in personal conversations. Some said it was a wonderful opportunity for
me to carry to a logical conclusion the work I had been doing. Others
warned me against even considering the possibility of managing in the
minor leagues. They gave many reasons, but the one which stuck in my
mind was that it would be a dead end street for me, that I would never
manage in the majors.

Well, why can't I manage in the majors? Because I am a Negro?
Because I am emotional? Because I can't get along with people, no matter
what the pigmentation of their skin? Because white players would resent
me and would be reluctant to take orders from me? Because baseball isn't
ready now or never will be ready to accept a Negro as a manager at the
major league level? Because I'm not qualified by experience or ability?

To all these questions, except possibly the last—which I would be
sure to prove—I say nuts! Ten years ago there were people who said I
wouldn't be accepted in organized baseball, and that I couldn't make it
in the majors. On the one hand, the inherent decency of the majority
of our population proved them wrong. On the other, I think I can mod-
estly say I helped to prove them wrong.

I was the first Negro player and I certainly wasn't the last. The doors
of the big leagues are opened wide now for any man who is qualified for
any job that has to be filled. With pride I say I had a hand in that. With
pride, too, I say I can manage in the majors.[6]

6. Jackie Robinson, as told to Milton Gross, "Why Can't I Manage in the Majors?,"
miscellaneous clipping (1956), JRP, box 1.

Robinson concluded the interview by pointing to the example of his mentor: "All that's needed for the next barrier to be broken down is for somebody with the courage, conviction and foresight that Mr. Rickey had to go ahead and do it."

In the following column, Robinson continues to criticize the absence of black managers in Major League Baseball. Interestingly, he does so by appealing to a racially progressive action undertaken by President John Kennedy. Robinson had publicly opposed Kennedy's candidacy for high office, primarily because he had found the Massachusetts senator to be unfamiliar with black concerns. But Robinson's assessment changed markedly on June 11, 1963, when President Kennedy, shocked by racial violence in Birmingham, Alabama, delivered a nationally televised, and moving, civil rights speech promising additional civil rights reforms.

Source: New York Amsterdam News, *February 24, 1968, 17.*

WHEN THE LATE John F. Kennedy was reviewing the colorful ceremony of his own inauguration, he spotted a colorful contingent of special honor guardsmen in the line of march. President Kennedy made a mental note of a fact which disturbed him. The group of soldiers was a lily-white group. One of Mr. Kennedy's first acts in office was to summon high Army officials to the White House.

In response to his question about the lack of Negroes in the honor guard, the high Army officials explained that this particular unit was an elite one with extremely difficult standards of qualification.

"You see, Mr. President," they declared, "Negroes just do not apply."

The President's reaction was swift and curt.

"Go out and get some," he ordered.

You will recall that heart-wrenching sight when John Kennedy's lifeless body was tenderly transported through the streets of the nation's capital. In all honor guard contingents, black young men marched, straight and tall—every inch as fine soldiers as their fellows.

To be aware of a story of such beautiful, simple justice as the above is to make one almost wish to throw up when one recalls the kind of garbage which is attributed to Larry McPhail, the general manager of the Yankees.

In a piece in the *New York Post*, writer Maury Allen discusses the well-known truth that minority baseball players, no matter how much they put out for the game, get bypassed when it comes to jobs in the front office. Negro players play their hearts out. But when their popularity or their best playing days are over, there is just no room for them in the executive suite.

Allen points out that there are no Negroes working in front-office jobs for either of the New York clubs. Allen quotes McPhail, the Yankees general manager, as saying:

"There are very few jobs in the front office of baseball. There is also a very small amount of turnover. It is very difficult to find qualified Negroes with the right educational background for front-office jobs."

The clubs spend all kinds of money, time and effort scouting for talent. Yet, they find it "difficult" to look right over their noses to discover quite a few articulate, intelligent players who could fit ably into administration.

Robinson would not live to see the first African American manager in Major League Baseball, but he continued to express his thoughts on the matter until just before his death.

On October 15, 1972, he threw out the ceremonial first ball of the second game of the World Series, marking the twenty-fifth anniversary of his role in shattering the color barrier, but he did not agree to do so until baseball commissioner Bowie Kuhn had assured him that Major League Baseball was taking concrete steps toward hiring African Americans for management positions. And then, when he made his speech at the ceremony, Robinson stated: "I am extremely proud and pleased to be here this afternoon but must admit I'm going to be tremendously more pleased and more proud when I look at that third base coaching line one day and see a black face managing in baseball."[7]

Robinson died of complications from diabetes nine days later.

---

7. Quoted in Rampersad, *Jackie Robinson: A Biography*, 459. A transcript of these comments is available in the JRP, and footage of the event, along with Jackie's televised comments, is accessible online at YouTube.com and Biography.com.

Frank Robinson, no relation to Jackie, became the first African American manager in Major League Baseball when he took the reins of the Cleveland Indians in 1975.

No More Turning the Other Cheek
The Real Jackie Robinson

Dick Young, a sports reporter and columnist for the "New York Daily News," wrote some rather harsh words about Robinson after Jackie had publicly stated that Willie Mays and other African American athletes were not doing all they could to advance civil rights in the United States. "There is much to admire in Jackie Robinson, and there is much to worry about," Young wrote. "His conception of his infallibility is the thing that always made me wonder most. Anybody who doesn't do things Jackie Robinson's way is wrong. He has always believed this and evidently he hasn't outgrown such immature adamance. . . . One of the things I most admire in Jackie Robinson is his restraint. He hasn't yet called Willie Mays bigoted for disagreeing with him."[8]
Source: New York Amsterdam News, March 30, 1960, 15.

LATE IN MY BASEBALL CAREER, after I had been through the mill as a target of name-calling, dirty tactics, and humiliation, Mr. Branch Rickey decided that his bold experiment was working. Baseball had become integrated and would never revert to being a game which excluded Negroes and Puerto Ricans. I could stop turning the other cheek. I could act and react just like anyone else in the game. I resolved not to take unfair advantage of my new freedom.

But when I felt an injustice was being done, I sounded off. When someone ridiculed me, I let him have as good as he sent.

There were many people who had praised me for my ability to "grin and bear it." Some of these same people became very disturbed when I

---

8. Dick Young, "Young Ideas," *New York Amsterdam News* (NYAN), March 22, 1968, 93.

began to speak my mind. In their opinion, I had become arrogant. I was—in their book—given to "popping off." I was now a hothead—to hear them tell it. Among these disturbed was sportswriter Dick Young.

Dick warned me that I must not be so articulate. He advised that, if I continued to protest, I would alienate the sportswriters. And they, after all, were the ones who decided who would get the various awards and honors in sports.

I tried to explain to Dick that, while I appreciate awards as much as the next man, no award could compensate me for failing to be true to myself and my convictions. The day that I can't look in the mirror without feeling ashamed of doing something phony or failing to tell it as I see it—simply to please others—that is a day I never want to experience.

Dick Young never did get my point. He never forgave me for not taking his advice. Throughout the years, whenever he thought he saw an opening, he has used his sports column to try to lecture me. The latest lecture refers to a television interview I had in San Francisco. I was asked a question about a subject which I did not introduce. Pat Collins, the interviewer, expressed the opinion that it appeared Willie Mays and other athletes were not doing enough for civil rights. She asked if I agreed. I do agree and I said so.

The next thing I knew there was a big, front-page headline in a leading San Francisco paper. The headline—which was not borne out by the story—claimed I had attacked Willie Mays on civil rights. Willie became angry and made a reply. Dick Young devoted a piece of his column to a blast, defending Willie and assailing me. Young said, among other things, that I call everyone who disagrees with me a bigot.

I consider Dick Young a bigot. I think he just doesn't understand. I think he is simply stupid about the truth concerning race relations. Dick liked the Jackie Robinson who couldn't answer back. He doesn't like the real Jackie Robinson. . . .

Time for Action Against the PGA

Golf was Robinson's second-favorite sport. He frequently hit the links at the municipal course in Stamford, and, according to television celebrity Ed

Sullivan, it seems Jackie had quite the swing. In written remarks for a din-
ner honoring Robinson, Sullivan fondly referred to Jackie as "my friend and
long-hitting golf partner."[9] Robinson frequently used his column to address
discrimination in golf, and in this one he attacks the Professional Golfers'
Association for not granting membership to African Americans.
Source: New York Post, February 24, 1960, 76.

GOLF IS THE ONE MAJOR SPORT in America today in which rank and open racial prejudice is allowed to reign supreme. Though often called the sport of gentlemen, all too often golf courses, clubs and tournaments apply the ungentlemanly and un-American yardstick of race and color in determining who may or may not compete.

Even the president of the United States, Dwight D. Eisenhower, holds membership in a golf club which limits membership to "Caucasians only"—the Augusta National Golf Club, where the Masters Tournament is held each year. And another famous and highly honored American, Bing Crosby, who annually sponsors a golf tournament bearing his name at Pebble Beach, California, has consistently refused to invite Negro professionals to compete.

I discussed this situation recently with singer Billy Eckstine, who is a fine golfer himself and a close friend of Charlie Sifford, the top Negro golfer around. Billy told me what happened when Charlie sought to enter the Palm Springs Invitational. Charlie called him, on the verge of tears, explaining that without giving a single logical reason, the directors had refused to accept his application. Sifford sought Eckstine's advice—and also that of Joe Louis, who has been a close friend and sponsor as well—as to whether the time has come when a suit should be instituted against the Professional Golfers Assn., which, with its own Caucasian clause, is often used as an escape by those who wish to avoid recognizing Negroes in golf.

Undoubtedly, the time has come for action. A number of golfers with less of a record than Sifford's were admitted to the Palm Springs

9. Ed Sullivan, "Tribute to a Golf Partner," Southern Christian Leadership Conference Papers, microfilm edition, part 12, 14:886.

tournament, and there is no reason other than his race that Charlie was refused. Since Charlie is endeavoring to make a living at his chosen craft, it constitutes a basic denial of economic opportunity when he is barred from membership in the PGA and from participating in many of the money tournaments. Not only should court action be considered, but I feel the issue is one for a thorough investigation by the Civil Rights Commission.

As I pointed out in this space just last week, the annual Baseball Players Golf Tournament sponsored by the deep Southern city of Miami has been admitting Negro players for years. In fact, George Jacobus, director of the tournament, told me the presence of Negro players has added immeasurably to the success and popularity of the event. If this is true in Miami, Florida, why couldn't the same be true in Palm Springs or Pebble Beach, California, or on the green where the president of the U.S. plays golf? . . .

I see no reason for this issue to be postponed. Sifford, Ted Rhodes and other Negro professional golfers should be judged right now on their ability alone. As proven golfers, they should be allowed—or "invited"—to participate in professional tournaments on exactly the same basis as everyone else. And membership qualifications which discriminate on the basis of the color of a golfer's skin rather than his score on the course should have no place in the PGA, in President Eisenhower's golf club, or anywhere else in American golf.

Cracking the Color Barrier in the PGA

With help from Robinson's public criticism of the Professional Golfers' Association, Charlie Sifford broke the color barrier in professional golf in March 1960, becoming the first African American member of the PGA.
Source: New York Post, March 30, 1960, 96.

CHARLIE SIFFORD phoned me from California yesterday to say: "We did it!" Sifford, who is the top Negro golf pro but who has been barred from many tournaments for lack of approval by the Professional Golfers Assn., told me he had just had word that his "approved player" card is on the way.

J. Edward Carter, managing director of the PGA, had called him, Charlie told me, to inform him that his application has finally been accepted by the PGA's executive committee. Carter said they had read my recent columns reporting on bias in golf, which particularly took the PGA to task for refusing Charlie the recognition he must have in order to pursue a career and livelihood in this field. "Robinson hit us pretty hard, didn't he?" Sifford reports Carter asked him, but added that I had hit the nail right on the head.

Sifford also reported that in their conversation Carter told him a North Carolina professional, Dugan Aycock, had particularly gone to bat for Charlie. Aycock, who is on the PGA's executive committee, stated he had known Sifford for a long time, that Charlie had caddied for him when only 10-years-old and that Sifford is a fine golfer who deserves to be accorded the right to play in PGA-regulated tournaments. There would undoubtedly be problems in some of the Southern states, Carter continued, but added that he would serve as Sifford's personal manager in such cases. He also volunteered to line up exhibitions to help Sifford financially.

I certainly want to convey my congratulations to the PGA for this historic step, as well as to Charlie Sifford for his long and gallant fight. Sifford thus becomes the first Negro professional golfer to be granted approved-player status, which is the first rung on the ladder to full membership in the PGA. And though the PGA has yet to remove the un-American "Caucasians only" clause concerning membership from its bylaws, I am greatly hopeful—now that the initial step has been taken—that the November PGA convention will do away once and for all with this bigoted requirement.

Robinson would continue to provide public support for Sifford's career. For instance, in February 1963 he called upon the readers of his column to boycott tire, car, and aluminum companies that sponsored celebrity golf television shows that did not include Sifford and other African American players. "Why should the buying power of our race be used to support manufacturers who do not give just due to the Negro?" Robinson wondered. "If the people who use these television shows to sell their products want to run Jim Crow shows, that's their business. But Negro people are suckers if they continue to

invest their spending dollars in Jim Crow. . . . Our race should learn to sup-
port its own. . . . Let's give our champions some real backing by refusing to
support businesses which choose to ignore our existence."[10]

A Shattered Dream

Private country clubs, like High Ridge Country Club in Stamford, Con-
necticut, barred Robinson from membership because of his race, and even
though he played at many of them as a guest, he resented the personal dis-
crimination and eventually sought to build his own club.
    Source: New York Amsterdam News, December 30, 1967, 13.

EVER SINCE I LEARNED to hit the golf ball, I have had a dream. . . .

I wanted to belong to a country club, bought or built by my own people. I wanted to be able to see my kids swimming in the pool, getting
acquainted with the children of my fellow members and developing the
kind of pride and assurance I've seen in other kids at country clubs where
I've been a guest, but where I would not have been accepted as a member.
I dreamed of a Charlie Sifford or a Ted Rhodes teaching golf to members
whose game needed polishing. I wanted to be able to provide the same
opportunities I see at so many other clubs.

I thought my dream was about to come true. I had called some friends
together and we assembled—over a period of months—what seemed to
be a promising group. One of the managers of a major bank had told me
he would be interested in granting bank loans to potential members on
an individual basis so long as they had the credit standing. I had negotiated with a group which owns a couple of hundred acres of land in a
picturesque Westchester spot. I thought I could see, in eighteen months, a
layout we would be so proud of.

Then the bubble burst. I met with the executive committee of the
group we had assembled. After looking over the contract and learning all

10. NYAN, February 23, 1963, 11.

the details, they told me in effect: "We're not ready for this." They didn't say it in so many words, but the defeatism was there. In their view, we would not get sufficient support until the course had been created and the clubhouse built. . . .

I must confess that I became disgusted. . . . I believe that we, as Negroes, are ready for such a project. We have a sufficient number of persons who love the game, who can afford the modest investment and dues involved, and who would be able to strengthen their family life, indulge more comfortably and consistently in this recreational activity and to further their business interests—provided they invest a little money and a lot more faith in themselves. . . .

I don't want to give up. But it gets to be like bumping your head against a brick wall. You bump and bump and all you get is a headache. While on the verge of throwing in the towel, I think I will still cherish my dream. One day it might come true. One day I will proudly belong to a group which will unite to do something constructive. We will create something which is a showplace of achievement. We won't have to depend on patronizing invitations. For you see that beautiful property over there? That is ours. We sacrificed for it. Isn't it beautiful? And above all, isn't it ours?

2

On Family and Friends

If It Makes Rachel Happy

In 1955 Robinson wrote a series of three articles for "Look," one of the most popular magazines in the country, and below is an excerpt from the one titled "Now I Know Why They Boo Me." Accompanying the article was a photo of the Robinson family standing in front of their new home in Stamford, Connecticut. Although he is sometimes depicted as a rugged individualist, Robinson saw himself as heavily indebted to many people, especially his mother, Mallie, and his wife, Rachel.
Source: Look, January 25, 1955, 23–28.

. . . RACHEL AND I often talk about those first hard days in baseball, and especially about the way baseball has changed our lives—and the lives of our three children.

My own childhood is one reason I try to win all the time. When I was 1-year-old, my mother was left alone on a farm in Georgia with five small children. I've never seen my father. My mother took us in dirty Jim Crow coaches to Pasadena, Calif., and raised us there. We lived in a house on Pepper Street on what money she was able to earn by working as a domestic servant.

We never had much to eat, except for day-old bread that we dunked in sugar and milk. Even now, Rachel has to remind me to eat green vegetables—I do as an example for our family—but I never developed a taste for them because I never ate them as a youngster. We had meat on Sundays only when my mother was able to get extra work. I was the youngest in the family, and my sister, Willa Mae, who is two years older, took care of me when my mother was working. When she went to school, I went along and played alone in the sandbox in the school until she got out of class.

The school authorities complained to my mother about this, for I was only 3-years-old, and they didn't want me on their hands.

"If I quit working to stay home to take care of him, I'll have to go on relief," my mother told them. "It'll be cheaper for the city if you just let him play in that sandbox."

So I stayed in the sandbox. When I was old enough to go to school myself, I told my mother she could save food by not fixing a lunch for me. I was the best athlete in class; the other boys brought me sandwiches and dimes for the movies just so they could play on my team. So you might say that I turned professional at an early age and that I had to win from the start if I wanted to eat. . . .

I can't help remembering those days, and maybe those people who are criticizing me for building a new house in Connecticut don't know about the years I spent in a sandbox waiting for my sister. . . .

But in moving away from the mixed Negro and white section of St. Albans, where we had lived for six years, we are not trying to escape our own race. No Negro with a family of growing children likes the idea of settling in a town like North Stamford, where there are no other Negro children. But we wanted Jackie, Sharon and David to grow up in the country instead of a crowded city. And where in the countryside of Westchester County in New York or Connecticut could we find a Negro neighborhood? There just isn't any. . . .

Last year we finally found a piece of land in Westchester County that was just what we wanted. We offered the owner his asking price; it was much more than he had expected to get for it. We waited a long time for a reply after our first offer. Then he told us that the price had been raised $5,000. We said we'd be glad to pay the extra $5,000. There was another period of confused silence. At last, we were told that the land had been sold to someone else. Everywhere we went it was like that.

Then a newspaper in Bridgeport, Conn., published a story saying that we wanted to buy some land in North Stamford, that we had been turned away because of our color. This was not really accurate. True, we had looked in North Stamford, but we had not seen anything we liked and it was only one of many towns where we had looked. But when the story appeared in the newspaper, the North Stamford people became indignant. Ministers delivered sermons on racial prejudice. A group of people in Stamford arranged for Rachel to look at every bit of property for sale in the area. Among the places shown was an eight-acre tract that matched her dreams. The setting, with lakes and trees, was just what she had always wanted, and we bought it. . . .

If there were other Negroes in North Stamford, we might have been able to build a smaller and less expensive house. We don't want our children growing up and not knowing Negroes of their own age. Rachel and I want our daughter and our sons to meet and know people of all races. There have been times when friends have asked us about the wisdom of mixed marriages and we have always told them that this is a matter between two individuals. We think that our own children must make their own choice and that we must help them once they have done so. We do feel that they would be happier by marrying within their own race. . . .

I feel that the house in Connecticut will be worth whatever it costs if it makes Rachel happy. Her patience and understanding enabled me to survive the loneliness of the times when I was the only Negro player at Montreal and Brooklyn. That first year, she was going through a difficult pregnancy, but I never knew it until years later. She said she didn't want to bother me because I was having my own problems. . . .

Our Children Need More than Material Things

Robinson wrote more than a few columns on the issue of juvenile delinquency, and never once did he condemn troubled children and youth. Instead, he was always on the lookout for concrete—and family- and community-based—ways to improve the lives of troubled youngsters. As a youth, Robinson himself had landed in trouble with the Pasadena police several times for minor infractions, and he often credited three community individuals for helping him to avoid more serious problems—Hugh Morgan, who headed the youth division of the Pasadena police force; Carl Anderson, a local mechanic who encouraged him to leave behind the Pepper Street

*Gang in his local neighborhood; and the Reverend Karl Downs, a minister
who took a keen interest in Robinson, even recruiting him to teach Sunday
school at Scott Methodist Church.*

Source: New York Post, *May 5, 1959, 80.*

I READ THE OTHER DAY that one out of every five youngsters in the
country between the ages of 10 and 17 has had some brush with the law.

Certainly, this is very shocking. Our juvenile delinquency is high, and
growing higher every year. It's frightening to think that sooner or later one
of your own children, or one of the neighbor's, or one of your relatives'
youngsters, will wind up in a police station charged with some offense
against the public good.

. . . [T]he real job in preventing the "JD" rate from continuing to rise
is to find ways of keeping kids from getting into trouble in the first place.

And in that connection, I'm concerned because we don't have enough
Dorothy Gordons around who recognize the importance of giving credit
to youngsters for just being what they are—young people, with the accent
on people. Miss Gordon, who conducts "The New York Times Youth
Forum" on TV, devotes a great deal of time encouraging youngsters, not
only through her program, but also in her spare time.

I think she's built up a very effective way of reaching and dealing with
kids by simply recognizing them as individuals, just as adults like to be
recognized. They're not just a "bunch of holy terrors" to her; they're Mary
and Jonathan and Kim and David—each different, each with his own set
of problems and reactions and talents. And each to be dealt with as a *person* seeking adult recognition of his differences.

Another example of what working with our youngsters can do is the
work of our minister here in Stamford, Conn. There used to be groups of
kids who got into trouble, doing little things that could have led to big-
ger crimes. But since Rev. Osborne has been working with them in the
church and community center, there's a lot less talk about juvenile problems in our area today.

Rev. Osborne feels we are reversing the realm of responsibility of our
youngsters. There's too much emphasis, he says, on what we can do for our
kids, instead of what our kids can do for themselves. . . . [H]e suggests that

getting them to come to the church, the temple and the community center at an early age is the best possible way of keeping them out of difficulty.

I think this is good advice for all communities. Interesting our children in worthwhile community activities while they are still small—and seeing to it that we participate with them—will go a long way to ensure that none of our children turns up as a statistic on the JD report of next year, or the years after that.

Of course, some people have excuses as to why they can't get around to doing this. But these are the parents we most often hear say: "Why did he do a thing like this? We give him everything at home—we work hard to get him anything he asks for. He had no reason to get into trouble!"

The trouble is, though the material things are well provided, the youngster needs more than this. He needs love and affection, of course, but perhaps most of all he needs his parents to recognize him and his problems as important. Every problem is a big one to a child. But how often do we come home from work, thinking we're providing well for our kids, and then slough them off with a quick answer or a tired excuse? This, more than anything else, is the answer to the parent who asks, "Why?" . . .

People Are People

Robinson addresses the issue of racial purity in relation to his friend Harry Belafonte, the first African American to win an Emmy. Belafonte won the distinguished honor in 1959 for his own television special, "Tonight with Harry Belafonte." The award-winning actor and singer was born in New York City, and during part of his childhood he lived with his maternal grandmother in Jamaica. Belafonte played a very active role in the civil rights movement, and in 1958 and 1959 he joined Robinson and Coretta Scott King in national marches for integrated schools; the marches were conceived and organized by Bayard Rustin, the main tactician of the movement, who frequently sought to enlist celebrities for the cause of civil rights. Robinson, as the following column suggests, was quick to offer a public defense of his friends, black and white, when he felt they were being unfairly attacked.
Source: New York Post, May 14, 1959, 84.

I CALLED HARRY BELAFONTE out in Las Vegas yesterday. I called to express my disgust over a hostile and unwarranted article. . . .

I wouldn't dignify the more obviously snide and intemperate attacks upon Harry by repeating them in this space. But I do have something to say about two points.

The . . . writer boldly states that Harry, not being what he calls a "pure Negro," could never identify himself with other Negroes. Well, I don't know just what he means by "pure Negro." I also don't know what is meant by pure white. An anthropologist recently estimated that as high as 65 percent of all so-called "white" Americans have some Negro ancestry, whether they know it or not. Likewise, the cruelties of slavery in America have resulted in a high percentage of Negroes with varying degrees of white genes.

To me, however, neither of these is of the least importance whatsoever. People are people, no matter what race or color they or their grandparents are, and must be evaluated for themselves, not on the basis of their "blood."

I've had the pleasure of knowing Harry Belafonte for a number of years now. Shoulder to shoulder, we—and tens of thousands of others, Negro and white—have participated in two Youth Marches for Integration to Washington. I've heard him speak, publicly and privately, on many occasions on behalf of Negro causes and benefits. And Harry takes particular pains to make public at all times his identification with the NAACP, recognizing that his success places him in a favorable position to be listened to in promoting justice and equal rights for others less fortunate than he.

Also, a great deal of Harry's song material springs from Negro life and folklore, both here and in the West Indies. So if Harry "wants to be white," as the writer quotes one source as saying, he certainly picks a strange way of going about it.

I've often noticed that any Negro who shows the kind of militant, uncompromising attitude Harry does on basic human rights lets himself in for charges such as these. But the fact is, wanting and demanding equal treatment do not in the least imply giving up an identification with others who are also non-white. In fact, as Martin Luther King recently pointed out, over three-quarters of the world's population is non-white. And with freedom on the march everywhere, it's getting to be more and more fashionable *not* to be white! . . .

Santa Robinson

The following column, as well as the images it calls to mind, is among the best evidence for demonstrating that even in public Jackie Robinson was more than the fiery prophet who criticized public figures. If anyone saw Robinson's tenderness in public settings, it was the many children who ran by his side to get his autograph, to touch him, or just to be near him; they brought him as much joy as politicians caused him pain.
Source: New York Post, *December 28, 1959, 64.*

ONCE AGAIN, Christmas was a happy occasion for us at the Robinson household. My wife Rae and I got a great deal of pleasure out of watching our youngsters, Jack, Sharon, and David, exchange gifts and share in that wonderful feeling of having given a gift, no matter how small, to please someone else.

I was particularly proud this year that my oldest son had grown to the point that he wanted to earn his own money for presents. And although I knew each of the kids expected gifts in return, I think in large measure the true spirit of giving at Christmas managed to prevail.

As much as I enjoyed our family Christmas, still I don't know if it was any more of a thrill than the opportunity I had in playing Santa Claus this year for the N.Y. Herald Tribune Fresh Air Fund. Now, playing Santa to some 266 boys and girls is not an easy role. It required my talking with, and handing out presents to, each of these kids, and believe me, it got rather uncomfortable in that hangar at Idlewild Airport under that long beard, red suit, and all those pillows!

"Santa" arrived in an airplane, and I confess I was more than a little anxious as we taxied toward the hangar and through the window I could see all those kids excitedly awaiting Santa's appearance. Though I've been lucky enough to experience an ovation or two on the baseball diamond, I can honestly say I'd never heard anything like the roar that greeted me as I stepped off that plane. There was a momentary fear when one youngster shouted: "Hi, Jackie Robinson—you can't fool me!" But the other kids either didn't hear or didn't care as they surged around Santa in excitement and joy. . . .

Out at the airport, as each youngster came up to talk to Santa, I had a more than uneasy feeling. In somewhat of an unsure manner, one would say, "Santa, may I have a bike?"—or a doll, a train, or some other gift he had long dreamed about and set his heart on. How do you promise a child a present that may never come? I thought of how wonderful it would have been if Santa could have assured them through the Fund that each would receive the one gift he wanted most.

Unfortunately, this could not be done, and all Santa could say was that he would talk with their parents to see if the children had been good boys and girls, and perhaps their presents would come. It was a feeling of sadness, but one of great happiness, too, as I watched each child go away with hope dancing in his eyes.

Great credit is due to all those who have made the Fresh Air Fund such a success. Regardless of how small my contribution may have been, I got a big kick out of giving of myself at this affair, and those who have helped financially may well feel proud also. Regardless of the size of the donation, each contributor has shared in giving a needy child a larger measure of hope. And hope, after all, is the greatest gift of all at Christmastime.

What about Interracial Marriages?

In a case that attracted national attention, Dorothy Lebohner, a white cheerleader, and Warren Sutton, an African American basketball player, met and fell in love in the late 1950s at Alfred University in New York—a school that extolled its commitment to nondiscrimination in its catalog. But Lebohner's father, Edward, who also served as the college's bursar, was displeased with the interracial relationship and sought to squelch it in a variety of ways. Indeed, because of pressure applied by Edward Lebohner, Sutton left the college under duress before graduating.

Dorothy and Warren remained in touch, however, even as her father persisted in trying to break them up. One of his schemes in early 1960 was to send her to Florida for an extended stay. But the resourceful Dorothy slipped out of her New York City hotel room just before she was to travel South and met up with Warren for nearly a full day of roaming around the city and enjoying each other's company. Her parents called the police after becoming worried and consented to their daughter being arrested as a "wayward minor" when she and Warren were discovered watching a movie in the city. The two pledged their love for each other at the police station, and Edward Lebohner took the occasion to announce his opposition to interracial marriages. "Many of her friends are amazed at our opposition to this romance," he stated. "But this integration stuff has its limits. Mixed marriages don't work."[1]

Source: New York Post, February 8, 1960, 52.

THE CASE OF THE ALFRED UNIVERSITY COED whose father had her picked up last week on a warrant branding her a "wayward minor" for continuing to see a Negro basketball star to whom she is engaged raises some interesting and serious questions. For one of the old, standby buga-boos often used as a last resort by opponents of equal rights for Negroes is: "How would you like your daughter to marry a Negro?"

Raising the specter of wholesale, interracial marriage is, of course, a feeble argument at best. For, considering the general state of racial atti-tudes in this country, it seems quite safe to assume that, by and large, Negroes will continue to marry Negroes and whites to marry whites. Breaking down the bars of segregation and discrimination has never yet resulted in any high degree of interracial marriage, North or South, and for anyone to use this argument to continue to deny others equal rights and opportunities is just plain deceitful.

Still, there are instances of marriage between members of different races in America, and the first thing to be recognized is that these, gener-ally, are not "shotgun weddings." Nobody forces the participants to the altar or the magistrate; they go because each party wants to, just as most other people do. And though it may be difficult for some people to accept the fact that individuals of differing races may fall in love with each other

---

1. "Education: The Bursar's Daughter," *Time*, February 15, 1960, http://www.time .com/time/magazine/article/0,9171,871482,00.html.

and want to spend their lives together, it can and does happen, and there is no reason whatsoever to apologize for it.

Marriage between any two parties is a greatly personal thing which by and large is nobody else's business. It is they who will be living together, not their in-laws or other relatives, and thus it seems to me highly presumptive on anyone else's part to tell them whom they should or should not marry. The most that any outsider has any right to do—including their parents—is, it seems to me, to discuss the practicalities of the situation and offer their advice. But the final decision in a free society must lie with the parties involved, and if they decide that they are truly in love and wish to take their chances, then no one else has the moral right to interfere.

Unquestionably, there are special problems which two young people of differing races face in considering marriage, and each must be mature enough to realize that it will take a special effort to cope with them. But the statement made by this girl's father—"I know mixed marriages are almost impossible"—is simply not true. I know quite a number of such couples who lead full and happy lives raising their families and going about their normal pursuits without any of the catastrophes often predicted for interracial marriage.

Some are very outstanding people. Others are quite ordinary. But all are mature enough to have recognized, and conquered, the special problems which they faced, and now are easily able to take life in stride just as any other couple does. Many have excellent relations with their parents and in-laws, as well as with the people in their communities, and the subject of their differing races hardly ever has reason to come up. Their children grow up and play with other children the same as others do, with few if any special problems resulting from it.

There are other couples, of course, who should never have gotten married in the first place—but that is true of marriage in general. The important thing is that the two parties have a strong foundation of love for one another, and that they be mature enough to realize in advance what problems would arise and be ready to cope with them if they do.

From reports, this has been true with Dorothy Lebohner and Warren Sutton. Sutton has told of how both tried to withstand their growing love for one another for quite a time, but eventually faced up to it and began to lay plans for eventual marriage. Even with Sutton forced to leave school by steady pressure from the girl's father and other university officials, their love for each other has held up. It seems plain that her father's actions in forcing Sutton out of school contributed to her own in meeting him in secret. The father has but himself to blame, especially now that he has compounded the crime by branding her a "wayward minor" before all society.

I have no way of knowing whether these particular two young people can make a go of eventual marriage or not. Certainly, both should try to finish their educations before any such action is taken. But I submit that their parents have no way of knowing that they can't. The fact that these two are of differing races seems to me a minor problem of little significance. If they are mature enough as individuals to face life together, then they should be allowed the same chance at happiness that their parents took when they themselves got married.

Dorothy and Warren eventually married, but not with the approval of her father. Ever insistent, he sought to have the marriage annulled. But he failed in that effort.

The Most Important Person in My Life

Robinson focuses here on the supportive role that Rachel played during his baseball career, describing her as a "full partner" in all of his life endeavors. Beyond home plate, Rachel and Jackie partnered together in supporting the civil rights movement by hosting "An Afternoon of Jazz," a fund-raising event they held many times at their pastoral home in Stamford, Connecticut. These events played a very important role in bringing together various civil rights factions—including the NAACP and the Southern Christian Leadership Conference (SCLC)—for a strong show of unity. While Rachel played an active role in Robinson's professional career, their family life, and even the wider civil rights movement, she also flourished in her chosen career in professional nursing, eventually landing a faculty position at the prestigious Yale University School of Nursing.

Source: *New York Amsterdam News*, February 10, 1962, 9.

WHEN I WAS A STUDENT at the University of California, a friend introduced me to a pretty brown girl named Rachel Isum. Often now, I wonder where I would be in life and what would have happened to me if I hadn't met Rae—who is now Mrs. Jackie Robinson.

One thing I know for certain. I can't imagine how I would have made it through the bad days or the good if it hadn't been for the understanding, love and devotion she has given me down the years.

For two reasons, we almost goofed back in those early days. We almost goofed and didn't get married.

The first reason was that Rae did not—as the storybooks go—fall in love with me at first sight. In fact, she told a friend of hers that she thought I was conceited. I guess she thought it had gone to my head that I was pretty much of a campus celebrity because of my sports record at UCLA. She found out later, however, that I wasn't as much conceited as I was withdrawn and sort of sick of people who raved over you today because you were a campus hero and who actually liked you as much as they liked your last sports victory.

After Rae and I became engaged and while I was in the service, we almost goofed again. We had one of those silly lovers' quarrels. Rae wrote me and told me she wanted to volunteer for the service. I wrote back and told her she was my personal draftee—so please stay home. She even returned my ring and we both thought it was all over.

If it hadn't been for my mother, the other great influence in my life, it might have been over. Mothers don't mind telling you the truth. So, when I went home on furlough, miserable because I was in Los Angeles and Rae was in San Francisco and we were worlds apart, my mother said: "Jackie, call Rae. You know that's what you want to do."

Rae and I made up. Although, like all normal couples, we've had our minor spats and problems, we haven't ever become estranged from each other again.

I'm sure we never will.

There is so much that I owe to Rae that life without her just wouldn't seem to make sense. She has been my critic, my companion, my comforter and inspiration. She was the force behind my drive to make good in the world of sports and she is the force behind my drive today to make good in the world of business. She has been a sweet wife and a loving mother to our three children.

Thinking about Rae always makes me want to remind girls and women how important they are in making the world go round. It's an old saying—but a true one—that behind every successful man there is usually a woman who deserves much credit for his success.

I recall the days at ballparks, all over America, when I got a hard way to go. I can remember being insulted by someone because of my race—or just having a bad day or a slump. Rae was always there when I got home. She was there to say exactly the right word or to kiss me and make me realize that, after all, the world hadn't come to an end.

In my trophy room at home, I've got lots of awards and medallions and certificates. Sometimes I think there should be two names on them instead of just mine. For Rae has been a full partner in anything I have done or tried to do ever since that lucky day in California when we decided to share our lives.

This Friday night, I'll be in Washington, D.C. to speak at a rally of the NAACP. Just as soon as it is over, I'm going to head straight for home. The next day, Saturday, is going to be a day dedicated to the most important person in my life. It will be our anniversary and I'll use every possible minute of it to say to Rae—as I say subconsciously every day—"thank you!"

Just Get a Little Closer

In this discussion about family challenges, Robinson is most likely alluding to struggles that he and Rachel sometimes faced when rearing their children. At this point, Jackie Jr. was having some trouble finding his way through life, and two years later he would be serving in the US Army. In an April 1965 letter to Branch Rickey, Robinson wrote: "Jackie, Jr. is in the army, and while he does not like it, we feel it's the best thing for him. He did not want to stay in school, and the army was the next best thing."[2] Jackie Jr. would earn a

2. Robinson to Branch Rickey, n.d. [received April 12, 1965], Branch Rickey Papers, box 24, folder 15, Library of Congress, Washington, DC.

Purple Heart in the Vietnam War, return to the United States with a drug addiction, and then begin to turn his life around before dying in a tragic car accident in 1971.

Source: New York Amsterdam News, January 19, 1963, 11.

. . . I DON'T OFTEN WRITE about highly personal things, but I'm anxious to let the world know that for my wife Rachel and me this holiday season turned out to be the most wonderful we've ever experienced.

I'm not speaking so much of the many cards and nice gifts which we received.

There was one gift which we wouldn't exchange for a million dollars.

Our three children—David, Sharon and Jackie, Jr.—presented us with a loving cup. On it were written the simple words: "To the best parents." Under this inscription were their names.

At our home in Connecticut, I have a trophy room in which I keep many mementos of my sports career—as well as plaques, awards and loving cups of all descriptions which have been given to me for work in the civil rights field after I left the game.

Among the most prized possessions in this trophy room are the NAACP's Spingarn, the Baseball Hall of Fame trophy, and the SCLC's 1962 Hall of Fame plaque.

Yet, honestly, I can say that Rae and I prize this loving cup we received from the youngsters above anything we have.

I develop this subject because I am hoping there will be a bit of help for others in my expression of the reason for our gratitude.

Let me not kid you for one moment. I don't want to pretend that all is perfect harmony and bliss at our home. Like any other family, we have our problems. Up until this Christmas, we haven't been sure we were even on our way to solving some of our problems.

The loving cup has given us hope that we may be able to make a great deal of progress in 1963.

We believe the solution to difficult family situations lies in the projection of love and kindness between children, parents and others who are in close contact. We also believe that casting one's bread upon the waters truly returns happiness to those who give as well as to those who receive.

Sitting down to our holiday meal, I found myself hoping and wishing that there could be more closeness among families—all kinds of families but particularly Negro families. I single out the Negro because we always hear so much about the high rate of crime in Negro communities.

Our leaders talk of the sources of that crime—job discrimination, overcrowding, segregation, neglect.

Usually, this criticism is leveled against white society for keeping the Negro within a walled fence—subtly in the North and openly in the South. While I feel this position is justified, I would like to say it is time for the Negro parent to take a long inward look in an attempt to find out how much he is responsible for.

You may live segregated, but you don't have to live without love in your home. You may be crowded into an overpriced, under-serviced apartment, but there's still room in your home for kids and grownups to try to help each other.

I have seen so much in the Harlem area—so much that points to the fact that, if our youngsters had the kind of home life they need and deserve, we'd have a lot less of them going around getting themselves into trouble.

I just wanted to say that I hope your 1963 will be just fine. I wanted to get over the thought that you can make it a better year for yourself and those close to you if you just get a little closer to them.

At the March with Rae and Our Children—Never Prouder

One of the hallmark characteristics of Robinson's civil rights work was his commitment to advancing economic opportunities for African Americans, and in August 1963 he and Rachel made sure to take their children to the March on Washington for Jobs and Freedom. Robinson understood the connection between his family life and his civil rights work as inextricable—he fought for first-class citizenship so that his children would be able to enjoy the rights and privileges long denied him. Robinson refers to Senator Strom Thurmond of South Carolina, Senator John Stennis of Mississippi, and Senator Russell Long of Louisiana—all of them segregationist southerners who were often on the receiving end of Robinson's righteous anger.

Source: *New York Amsterdam News*, September 7, 1963, 11.

WEDNESDAY, AUGUST 28, is certainly a day which will go down in history and which, for this writer, will remain a splendid memory.

I have never been so proud to be a Negro.

I have never been so proud to be an American. For the marvelous multitude which poured into Washington was as American as a ham sandwich. It was salt and pepper.

One had to be deeply moved as he stood, watching Negroes and whites, marching hand in hand, singing songs for freedom.

I have never been so proud of our noble national leaders as I was on Freedom Day in Washington.

I could have become discouraged, listening to three Southern senators who were interviewed on television and who gave their distorted reactions to the march. I could have been discouraged, realizing that the stupidity they displayed could come from the lips of men in such high places. Nothing could enhance the cause of the Negro more, I believe, than to have Dr. Martin Luther King, standing, erect and proud, making his classic and statesmanlike speech in which he says: "I have a dream. I have a dream, deeply rooted in the American dream. I have a dream that, one day, right down in Mississippi, little black girls and boys will walk together with little white girls and boys, as sisters and brothers. I have a dream that one day my four children will be judged not by the color of their skin but by the content of their character. I have a dream."

Nothing could enhance our cause more than to have this moving picture of a dedicated and eloquent man and to hear his words and then to see and hear the decadent, ignorant philosophy of Thurmond of South Carolina, Stennis of Mississippi and Long of Louisiana.

It seems unbelievable that, from the lips of a senator should come the observation that Negroes have *more* in this nation than anywhere else because they own television sets and automobiles. On one hand, this bigot speaks of TVs and cars, while on the other, 200,000, white and black, are talking and singing about dignity and justice. Telstar beamed that marvelous demonstration to the world. What a beautiful picture we marchers gave to the world. What an ugly one was sketched by those die-hard Senators who want things to remain as they have been.

While A. Philip Randolph, Roy Wilkins, Whitney Young and John Lewis did a great job, there is no denying that the statement of Dr. King— a statement which I believe will go down in history—keynoted not only the entire affair but also the mood of the Negro Revolution.

To me, there were so many personal thrills. There was the thrill of marching, hand-in-hand with my eleven-year-old, David, explaining to him who Rosa Parks was, how her refusal to move to the rear of a bus in Montgomery triggered a great movement; explaining to him how Daisy Bates had stood up for justice in Little Rock and could not be intimidated, even by the ominous crack of bullets; listening to David when a newspaperman asked what the March meant to him and hearing David reply that it had taught him the importance of people working together; seeing the tremendous excitement in the face of my wife, Rae, as Dr. King spoke his masterpiece; getting reports about my older son, Jackie, how he was singing and clapping, expressing his desire to be a part of this great movement; watching his concern as our daughter, Sharon, fainted and had to be escorted to a Red Cross station.

Yes, it was a great day. But as long as we have bigots in leadership like Stennis, Thurmond and Long, we will have a mighty task to accomplish. The attitude of these men makes it imperative that the great host of people in this country, who have come to see the meaning of this struggle, continue to march together, to sing together, to work and pray together and to go to jail together, as Dr. King says, so that one day we may proudly say we are all free at last. The attitude of these men certainly makes it imperative that the president exert pressure on Congress to see that meaningful civil rights legislation is not throttled. Should this happen and should we be forced to make a Freedom March through Alabama, as is being suggested by Rev. Fred Shuttlesworth, I am not so certain that nonviolence will win the day.

Ella Fitzgerald
Greater than the Greatest

Ella Fitzgerald, the "First Lady of Song," sent Robinson a check for one thousand dollars just after he announced in 1963 that he had accepted an invitation from Martin Luther King Jr. to join him in the civil rights campaign in Birmingham, Alabama. By the time Robinson wrote this column, Fitzgerald had already earned her well-deserved reputation as America's most popular singer. "A-Tisket, A-Tasket," a song she had cowritten with Al Feldman in 1938, became an enormous success and remains a classic in American music.

Source: New York Amsterdam News, February 22, 1964, 11.

JUST A FEW NIGHTS BACK, Rae and I found a really marvelous way of celebrating our eighteenth anniversary. Along with our dear friends Marian and Arthur Logan, we spent an evening at the Americana Hotel's Royal Bandbox where Ella Fitzgerald was holding court.

I use the phrase "holding court" deliberately because, if there is any such thing as genuine royalty in show business, Ella is it. Rachel and I— along with the Logans—agreed that it was a great evening. For one solid hour, this fantastic artist held the entire room spellbound. I can hardly find words adequate to describe her performance. Really, in order to know what I mean, you would have to catch it yourself. All of us had known, for many years, that Ella fits fully that extravagant show business description: "the greatest." But, if it is possible, the "greatest" has become even greater.

With all the infectious charm and that incredibly versatile talent which she has had for years, it seemed to us that this was a new Ella, with new and deeper dimensions. Some of that lovable shyness seems to be gone and, in its place, there seems to be a kind of pixie mischief. Ella's personality, always very warm, comes over in such a tremendous way that you just can't resist loving her. . . .

Leaving the Bandbox, I felt I hadn't said enough to Ella to thank her for a great experience and a rich evening.

I don't think the world has said enough to her.

How tragic that this undeniably superior talent, acclaimed as it is, is not presented more often on the screens of our television and our moving pictures. When will justice and good taste become the order of the day, not only at lunch counters and ballot boxes, [and not only] to the extent that a few bigoted advertising agencies and corporation board chairmen decree?

Until that day arrives, American cannot be said to be fulfilling its promise of fair play to its citizens. It is not so much the Ella Fitzgeralds who suffer because of this unreasonable and criminal discrimination. It is the vast public which is deprived, simply because our country has not yet grown up.

Negro Women Are the Backbone of the Freedom Movement

A little more than a decade prior to this column, Rosa Parks refused to surrender her seat on a segregated bus in Montgomery, Alabama—an event that led the local women's political caucus to assume a leading role in organizing a boycott against the bus company. In his own life, Robinson often paid tribute not only to folks like Rosa Parks but especially to Rachel and his mother, Mallie. Rachel has described Mrs. Robinson as the major influence in Jackie's life.

Source: New York Amsterdam News, May 28, 1966, 17.

THERE IS ONE CHARACTERISTIC of New Yorkers which I find very discomfiting. Perhaps it is more universal than that. But I seem to notice it more often in New York City. I am talking about the lack of courtesy to women on the part of males—boys and men—the kind of courtesy which, not too long ago, was almost automatic.

I see men in mad dashes to capture a taxicab before it reaches a lady who is waiting for it. I see men and boys rush to sit in subway seats, leaving women standing. I see pushing and shoving and a whole atmosphere of panic on subways during rush hour when women are manhandled with unbelievable roughness.

Maybe I am a little square. I grew up in a home where we loved and respected our mother and a home in which we were taught that due deference must be given to the ladies. I am fortunate enough to have a wife who has been my partner and helper and who is well-liked by virtually everyone with whom she comes into contact. I shudder to think of how I would feel or react if someone showed open disrespect to her. I think all of us should give some thought to the question, Are we going backwards in the recognition of the basic values of decency? Is the world atmosphere of atomic war giving us and our youngsters a "what the hell" kind of attitude toward life and toward the standards society used to cling to?

I hope this is not true—and I am particularly anxious to believe it is not true of the Negro male. Let us face it—Negro women have been the backbone of our freedom movement. They have carried more than their share of the load. For myself, I know that I would never have been able to make the kind of progress I have been able to make without the support, devotion and love of my Rachel. To my mother I owe the realization at an early age that no one individual is better than another. You work and strive and try to do the right thing and you have a pretty good chance to make it.

When I discuss this subject among friends—discourtesy to our ladies—some of them say to me: "Well, you know there are some of our ladies who lose respect because they do not carry themselves or conduct themselves in a manner to command respect." This cannot be refuted, but it is not true of the vast majority. So why shouldn't we men be grateful for our ladies and honor and respect them each and every day of our lives?

The Magical Miss Pearl Bailey

Pearl Bailey was a famous Broadway actress and singer whose friendly, folksy manner captured the hearts of white and black audiences alike. Rachel and Jackie Robinson demonstrated their public support not just for Bailey but also for numerous other African American personalities in arts and entertainment. In return, many of them offered their own support for the Robinsons as they undertook efforts to raise funds for the civil rights movement.
    Source: New York Amsterdam News, *March 9, 1968, 17.*

RECENTLY, RACHEL AND I, on our twenty-second wedding anniversary, celebrated by going to see "Hello, Dolly!" We couldn't have chosen a better way to spend that very special evening. "Hello, Dolly!" beyond a doubt, is brilliant, a new and rare experience in theatre.

Everything about it is a joy—the production, the direction, the cast from the unforgettable Pearl Bailey and the superb Cab Calloway, right on down to the least important player. In fact, I dislike using the words "least important" because one of the things that makes the show so outstanding is the spirit of unity which comes across the footlights to make everyone in this magic musical important.

Magic is the word for Miss Bailey. She casts a spell. Charming, mischievous, genuine and lovable, she does an incredible job. She has such fantastic support in the person of Cab Calloway, who has to be the only living man who discovered and drank deeply from the Fountain of Youth. Cab has a natural copyright on that unique style of singing and dancing and his innate acting ability. Cab's daughter, Chris, is a winner. She earns rich bursts of applause, not only for her considerable talent, but also for a quality of enthusiasm which is contagious. Emily Yancy, who plays Mrs. Malloy, is as beautiful as her performance is impressive.

"Dolly," as you know, has an all-Negro cast. It wasn't too long ago that some people would have regarded this fact as a step backward. But "Dolly" is a long leap forward. It is such a beautiful company with its combination of colors from fair, through yellow, tan, brown and black. The quality and creativity of the costuming enhances the picture.

If it sounds like I fell in love with "Dolly," well, I guess that's the way it is. My own dolly, Rachel, who always looks great to me, was just beautiful that evening too. She was radiant with pleasure about such wonderful entertainment and I suppose, like me, she was thinking back over the many happy highlights of our long and wonderful relationship—adding this to the treasury of souvenirs.

The climax—totally unexpected—came when Pearl Bailey summoned us to the stage and created an impromptu and hilarious third act. This was all so flattering and made me feel so humble and proud at the same time that I guess I just got flustered. Being flustered made me clumsy and nervous and, trying to keep up with things, I bumped into a pretty dancer and knocked her off her feet. Talk about being embarrassed. I kept apologizing and everyone kept assuring me that everything was all right.

Except for this unfortunate incident, what a beautiful, beautiful evening it was. The audience reaction was tremendous. People loved the production, not only for the talent, the visual pleasure and the music, but for what it was saying. It would have done your heart good to see how the audience stampeded down the aisles to acclaim Pearl Bailey, when it was over.

They wanted to touch her, to hold her hand to thank her for a great experience. As Pearl herself said, what a fine thing it would be if this kind of appreciation could be carried over into the real drama of everyday life—if people could just be given honor and love and praise because of their talent or their character and without regard to skin color or religious background.

What a marvelous thing it would be if "Hello, Dolly!" could play the streets, not only in the ghettos, but in all kinds of neighborhoods in New York, Chicago, Los Angeles, Detroit, Newark, South Carolina—and yes, even in Jackson, Mississippi. Or maybe, especially there.

Dad, When Are You Going to Get with It?

The following is part of a published interview that Robinson gave in 1969 as part of his work for a new franchise—Sea Host, Inc. Although he used the interview to talk primarily about his hope for the emergence of an African American middle class, Robinson addressed a wide variety of questions, including the one that prompted the answer below: "We hear that there's a generation gap in the white community; is this also true in the Negro community?" Robinson's answer refers to his daughter, Sharon; to Black Panther leader Eldridge Cleaver; and to Whitney Young of the National Urban League. Robinson accidentally errs below, too; it was a picture of Black Panther leader Huey Newton that was hanging in Sharon's room.

> Source: "Toward a Black Middle Class: Sea Host, Inc.,"
> interview with Jackie Robinson, *Fast Food: The Magazine of
> the Restaurant Business* (November 1969) (reprint), no page
> numbers. Accessed at the Jackie Robinson Papers, Library of
> Congress, Washington, DC.

YES, I HAVE THREE KIDS and they say to me, Dad, when are you going to get with it?

My daughter had a picture of Eldridge Cleaver in her room and I objected to it.

She said, "But it's my room." I said, "But it's my house, and I want that picture down."

Of course I caught the devil from my sons. But we sat down and talked about it. Too many of us are unwilling to talk things out with our kids and try to get our views across.

I object to our young people having heroes who have been involved with dope, or who have gone to prison. Let's not look up to guys because they make a lot of noise.

What I was trying to get across to my kids was that there are men like Whitney Young whom we ought to look to as heroes. Whitney Young, in my opinion, has learned more in the last three or four years about what is going on, and has done more, than all the Eldridge Cleavers and all the other guys, in terms of bettering our position. So why shouldn't Whitney Young be the hero of the black community rather than Eldridge Cleaver?

You know, if a guy goes out and shoots and kills a police officer, in too many areas he's a hero. Too many of our young people don't care whether or not a guy has committed a crime.

3

On Civil Rights

It Comes Down to You and Me

Robinson was a popular public speaker following his retirement from base-ball, and it was a role he relished. He loved meeting people, pricking their consciences, and encouraging them to keep their eyes on the prize of racial justice. The column below is especially remarkable because it includes a hopeful, and personal, word to those who become frustrated in their efforts to effect change.

Source: New York Post, June 10, 1959, 88.

IN OUR STRUGGLE for equal opportunity here in America, people very often ask: "What can I as an individual do to help?" For instance, I hear almost daily from both Negroes and whites who are anxious to be of some practical service in righting wrongs and opening doors.

Well, I'm no race relations advisor or sociological expert, and certainly don't claim to have all the answers. But for what it's worth, I sometimes try to make a few constructive suggestions to those who ask, "What can I do?" For despite the tremendous progress over the years that we can all point to with pride, it comes down to you and me as individuals to keep the ball rolling.

First, I think it's up to each of us individually to try to straighten out our own thinking as best we can. Since none of us lives in a vacuum, I'd venture to suggest that hardly any of us can lay claim to being completely unprejudiced about other races and religions. And I think once we recognize that fact, and begin trying to change it, we've taken a giant step in preparing ourselves to be of service.

Prejudice means pre-judgment. It means judging another person or group by what you've heard or by what you're afraid might be true, or by what in some cases you know is true of certain individuals, but which you apply from then on to everybody else in the same group. In short, it's like condemning and executing a man before you're sure that he might have committed a crime. So I think the first step for each of us, Negro or white, is to stop thinking in terms of what we've heard, or what our "friends" have told us, or in any of the other ways in which prejudice is planted and cultivated in our society—and instead make certain that we judge other people as individuals.

When I see a Negro being boisterous on a bus or subway, I resent other people treating me as if that one Negro was proof Negroes are alike. Likewise, when I see a drunken white man in the street, I would resent anyone suspecting all white people are drunkards. People are individuals, good, bad and indifferent, no matter what their race or color or creed. And the sooner we begin to apply this to our own everyday thinking, by assuming the other fellow has just as much on the ball as we have—unless and until he proves otherwise—then the sooner we can set out on the task of convincing others.

Secondly, I believe in the old adage that a picture is worth a thousand words. Taken a step further, a good example is worth a thousand sermons. So to those who ask, "What can I do?" I'd suggest being a good example in dealing with and talking about people of other groups. In your everyday dealings, show that you regard other people with exactly the same esteem and respect as you do your own group. Most people will respond to and follow a good example, even though they might not otherwise take the lead themselves.

Next, I'd have to emphasize that Rome wasn't built in a day. Nor is prejudice—in ourselves or in others—eradicated overnight. So don't get discouraged if you don't set the world on fire the first time you try. There will always be those who will try to hold you back, or who'll be upset because you don't "conform" to their own fears or prejudices or weaknesses. There'll be those who want you to "let George do it," or accuse you of ulterior motives because you insist upon doing to others as you would have them do to you.

But each of us must live with himself, first of all, and we mustn't expect to accomplish too much at one time. Progress in changing people's hearts is sometimes slow. But it's such a satisfaction when at last you begin to see it happen.

Lastly, we can't wait for it to happen before we support efforts now to remove the barriers created by prejudice. Though prejudice is a state of mind, a Jim Crow sign or practice is a very real thing. You'll find that often merely removing the sign or correcting the practice will lead to the kind of situation where states of mind will change of their own accord. I've had literally scores of Southern whites state to me that once they left the segregated South, they began to think for the first time of Negroes as fellow human beings because there were no separate facilities and no special treatment in the North.

Supporting groups and organizations like the NAACP, the National Urban League, the National Conference of Christians and Jews, the Anti-Defamation League, and others is another part of what we all can do. . . .

In Defense of Student Sit-Ins

On March 19, 1960, former president Harry Truman made the following comment on the student sit-ins under way throughout the South: "If anybody came to my store and tried to stop business, I'd throw him out. The Negro should behave himself and show he's a good citizen. Commonsense and goodwill can solve this whole thing."[1] Several days later, Truman reiterated his position after two officials of the Detroit NAACP had asked him about it. "I would do just what I said I would," the former president added. "NAACP is an organization which has been working for goodwill and commonsense in this situation which we are facing today. When they do things that cause people, who have been friendly to them as I have been, to feel

---

1. "Truman Says He'd Oust Disrupters in His Shop," *New York Times* (NYT), March 20, 1960, 50.

that they are doing the wrong thing, they are losing friends instead of mak-ing them."[2]

　　　　Source: *New York Post*, March 25, 1960, 96.

FORMER PRESIDENT TRUMAN'S OUTBURST at the NAACP is a sad commentary on the man who, in 1948, gained the whole world's respect for thrashing the Dixiecrats. That he should now choose to attack those who are so valiantly fighting bigotry, rather than the bigots themselves, is regrettable but insignificant. For Negro Americans are determined to obtain their full rights and human dignity no matter whose voice is raised against them.

　　If Truman really means that he would "throw out" any of the quiet, orderly, peaceful students for merely asking to be served at a public lunch counter, then I suggest he open an establishment and prepare to begin at once. It is not the students who are "stopping business" in these stores. The managements themselves have closed their counters, rather than choose to sell Negroes sandwiches as well as toothpaste.

　　In point of fact, Negroes in the South do not now have the oppor-tunity of "showing" they are good citizens—as if any American should be required to prove the point to begin with to receive his "inalienable rights." Barred from the basic right of a citizen—the vote—and hemmed in by restrictions on opportunities for education, jobs, housing, culture and every other activity, it is little short of amazing that Negroes have "behaved themselves" as well as they have. It is also ironic that Truman set up no such requirement before sending his "greetings" indiscriminately to millions of Negro Americans to fight and die for their country in World War II and Korea.

　　This corner can only point out that progress will not wait upon Harry Truman or anyone else. Our young people refuse to be contented with even Truman's patronizing gradualism. And it is exceedingly pathetic to hear a former President declare he would resort to violence to oppose chil-dren peacefully asking to buy ice cream at a soda fountain. . . .

2. "Truman Reiterates Views on Sit-Downs," *NYT*, March 25, 1960, 12.

Truman later added that he "wouldn't be surprised" to learn that the student sit-ins were "engineered by communists."³ As a fierce defender of youths engaged in civil rights campaigns, Robinson replied to Truman's allegation by depicting the former president as "senile."⁴

South Africa and American Apartheid

Robinson used his columns more than a few times to publicize the injustices he saw in South Africa, and he gave early public support to George Houser, the executive director of the American Committee on Africa, a watchdog group organized in part to monitor and fight apartheid in South Africa. The ACOA is arguably the most understudied, and underappreciated, civil rights group of the modern civil rights era.

Source: New York Post, April 11, 1960, 46.

THE TRAGIC EVENTS taking place in the Union of South Africa serve more than ever to point up what by now should be an age-old maxim: rule by fear and force invites fear and force in return. South African Prime Minister Hendrik Verwoerd, fanatic architect of apartheid who edited a pro-Nazi newspaper during World War II, has consistently condoned and defended last month's brutal killings, beatings and arrests of Africans. That he now lies in a Pretoria hospital with two bullets in his head, a boomerang victim of his own blueprint of violence, is therefore not surprising.

The fact that the bullets came from the pistol of one of South Africa's three million whites, rather than from among its twelve and a half million non-whites, is significant, however. At this writing, little more has been disclosed about the would-be assassin than that he is a wealthy white English-speaking farmer. But the whites, already traditionally divided into

---

3. "Truman Denies Sit-In Remarks," *NYT*, April 21, 1960, 23. See also "Truman Repeats Charge on Sit-Ins," *NYT*, June 13, 1960, 20.

4. *New York Post*, March 25, 1960, 96.

hostile camps of Afrikaans- and English-speaking citizens, are now sure to be torn with more suspicions, fears and alarms than ever before.

For not only must they fear the mounting anger, bitterness and hatred of the Africans whom they keep enslaved through naked force, but it now appears they cannot trust each other as well. In short, the assassination attempt seems to me to indicate a falling-out among thieves. If so, then what happens next is anyone's guess.

Violence in any situation is always to be regretted. It must be remembered, however, that the shooting of the Prime Minister is no more and no less to be regretted than the killings, beatings and jailings of Africans which Verwoerd's own government ordered and is still carrying out. Thus, along with the official regrets and get-well messages now arriving in Pretoria from the capitals of the world should go an urgent plea for South Africa to stop now and reverse itself before it invites a real bloodbath to begin.

Or is it already too late . . . ?

Here in the U.S., the battle against American apartheid goes on. The Senate finally ended its disgraceful spectacle on Friday by passing a weak voting rights bill which President Eisenhower says he is "happy" with. Whether Southern Negro voters will be happy to try to run this intricate gauntlet before gaining their constitutional right to cast ballots remains to be seen. But we can't have everything—at least the President is happy.

Sit-Ins Bring Back Memories of My Own Experience

In the following column, Robinson draws a connection between his decision to "turn the other cheek" when he broke into Major League Baseball and the nonviolence exercised by students in the sit-in movement of Nashville, Tennessee. The movement targeted segregated lunch counters in downtown Nashville from February to May 1960, and more than 150 students were arrested as they sat at the counters in protest. Echoing Robinson's actions in 1947, the student protesters refused to hit back when their prosegregationist opponents taunted and pummeled them during the successful campaign. Robinson refers below to Reverend James Lawson, the leader of the Nashville sit-ins, who offered nonviolent workshops to the young protesters.

Almost eight years after the publication of this column, Lawson would urge Martin Luther King Jr. to travel to Memphis and lend his support to sanitation workers in their strike against the city's leaders.

Source: New York Post, April 25, 1960, 68.

CBS IS TO BE CONGRATULATED for its thoughtful, enlightening and arresting report on lunch counter sit-ins, "Anatomy of a Demonstration," shown yesterday over the CBS television network. This, you may recall, is the report a CBS camera crew was filming in Nashville, when Tennessee Governor Ellington charged the network with "instigating" the student sit-ins so they could be filmed for the show, a charge which CBS has denied.

The program documented a workshop in the techniques of nonviolent resistance, the Gandhian method by which Negro Americans in the South are forging a new chapter in the struggle against human indignity. The CBS cameras followed each move, step by step, as a group of Negroes and whites prepared themselves for the antagonisms and possible violence they might meet as they sought service at lunch counters in the downtown area.

The volunteers not only discussed what might happen, but in a greatly interesting sequence, they set up a "sample" lunch counter, split themselves into two groups—the demonstrators and the harassers—and proceeded to test their own principles and personal fortitude by intentionally goading one another in the same manner in which they could expect to be intimidated while on an actual sit-in. The harassing group called the demonstrators vile names, hurled racial insults, blew smoke in their faces, and finally attacked one demonstrator physically by dragging him off his stool. The demonstrators followed the principles of nonviolence—even when beaten—by refusing to fight back.

Actually, this program brought back memories of my own experience in breaking into major league baseball, for this was exactly the principle which Mr. Rickey and I agreed upon for the first tough year with the Dodgers. I can testify to the fact that it was a lot harder to turn the other cheek and refuse to fight back than it would have been to exercise a normal reaction. But it works, because sooner or later it brings a sense of shame to those who attack you. And that sense of shame is often the beginning of progress.

The leader and teacher of the Nashville workshop was a former Vanderbilt University ministerial student, the Rev. James M. Lawson. Though he was scheduled to receive his doctorate from Vanderbilt's Divinity School this summer, he was summarily expelled when his part in the sit-ins was publicized. This has not deterred young Lawson in the least, however, for he has continued to teach the doctrine of peaceful non-cooperation with segregation. Lawson spent three years in India studying the Gandhi precepts first hand, and when accused of preaching a "foreign ideology," he agrees that this concept originated nearly 2,000 years ago in a place called Bethlehem.

The CBS documentary could not have failed to move any thinking viewer, and thus it came as no surprise that a CBS network station in Memphis refused to allow the show on its airwaves. As the old adage goes, there is nothing so dangerous as an idea whose time has come. That these protests and demonstrations are having a telling effect is well demonstrated by the lengths to which desperate segregationists are going to try to curb them—the mass arrests, the tear gas, the fire hoses and the beatings. But still they go on, and they are growing.

The simple reason may be found in the answer Lawson gave to an interviewer during the program. Lawson was asked if Negroes themselves had contributed to the present strife by errors in judgment or strategy. He replied: "Yes. We have sinned by cooperating with the evils of segregation for as long as we have."

Panting for Man-Tan

Robinson was not inclined to use humor in his column, and so this is a rare look at his ability to laugh in the face of injustices and indignities.
Source: New York Post, May 4, 1960, 96.

. . . I'VE BEEN AMUSED also by the television advertisements for a skin-darkening preparation called Man-Tan. If you were to believe the implications of these ads, no man with a pale white skin can expect to find romance any more. All the girls are just panting after the man with that brown-as-a-berry complexion. And if you weren't born with it, don't despair. It now comes in a bottle, complete with application instructions, and it's guaranteed not to wash off.

Correct me if I'm wrong, but I thought the basis of all this silly stuff called segregation was a difference in skin pigmentation. If I were the governor of Alabama or Mississippi, I'd call a special session of the legislature to pass hurry-up laws against this latest NAACP scheme for "mongrelization." Why, keep this kind of thing up, and a body won't know who to segregate anymore. . . .

Just How Important Is Civil Rights?

Although personally inclined toward the Republican Party, Robinson tended to side with whichever candidate he deemed most progressive in the field of civil rights. And in 1960 his preferred presidential candidate was Richard Nixon. The two had first met during the 1952 Republican National Convention in Chicago, where, in a private conversation with Robinson, Nixon recounted a particular play from a 1939 football game between UCLA and the University of Oregon; it was a play in which UCLA's star running back Jackie Robinson was the main actor. Robinson was dazzled by Nixon's memory of the game, and the two continued to be friendly in the following years.

Robinson grew to be especially impressed with Nixon's virulent anticommunism, his 1957 trip to Africa (during which he made pro–civil rights statements), his efforts in passing the Civil Rights Act of 1957, his stated eagerness to move faster on civil rights than President Eisenhower, and his selection of the racially progressive Henry Cabot Lodge Jr. as his running mate for the presidency. Conversely, Robinson found John Kennedy to be unfamiliar with black concerns and all too willing to curry the favor of segregationist Dixiecrats.

Source: New York Post, August 22, 1960, 48.

SATURDAY NIGHT, radio commentator Barry Gray and I had a discussion concerning what he has several times referred to as a "blind spot" that I and other Negro Americans supposedly have. Civil rights, Barry stated, is not the only issue in American life—in fact, he doubted if it was even the most important issue. I and other Negroes should think more often of the "long view," Barry told me, since our concentration upon this issue smacked of the same self-centered blindness that marked, for instance, the wealthy Texas oilman who thinks of nothing but his 27½ percent depletion allowance.

Barry is a longtime friend of mine, and I have always admired and respected his fearless outspokenness on any issue that interested him. But I suspect it may be Barry—and a lot of others like him—who should check their eye doctors for astigmatism.

It seems to me it is very easy to tell others to stop rocking the boat and concentrate on the passing scenery when you are comfortably riding inside and the "others" are struggling to get on board. It should take no special spectacles to be able to see that people who are barred—often by law—from full and equal participation in our national life are naturally going to be more concerned about removing those bars than they are in joining the debate over eliminating the national debt or what shall we do about Castro.

Those civil rights that Barry and a lot of letter-writers think are so unimportant just happen to be the ticket of admission to the starting line. There is nothing "luxury" about civil rights, and I can't help resenting the implication that Negroes can just as well do without them while we grapple with the "larger" problems of the country and the world. There would be no U.S. as we know it if everyone else were as deprived of their rights as millions of Negro Americans are, since freedom of the individual is the cornerstone of democracy.

It may be difficult for those who have never had to worry about those basic rights here in America to understand why those who do often concentrate upon the issue so much. But I challenge Barry and those others to stop and think: Suppose you were the father or mother of the two Negro children who lie in a hospital in Chattanooga, Tenn., today, innocent victims of concussion and flying glass when their home was bombed Saturday night? Would you go to work the next morning and chat pleasantly with your fellow workers about farm policy or labor legislation?

Or what if you were one of the scores of Negro Americans in Fayette County, Tenn., whose children are ill and undernourished because local merchants refuse to sell them even bread and milk because they sought to register to vote? How much interest could you muster in fiscal policies or protective tariffs?

In this political year, I find myself aware of each and every issue, just as any other American should be. But for those who question my consideration of candidates and parties primarily on civil rights grounds, I can only answer that this, for me—and for millions of other American voters—is the most important issue in the election since it is the very basis of our democracy. I'm grateful, of course, for the opportunities which I and others have had. But if anyone thinks this is going to make me turn my back on those who haven't had the same advantages, then I must repeat: I won't have it "made" until the most underprivileged Negro in Mississippi can live in equal dignity with anyone else in America.

It's Sad to Watch a House of God Die

Martin Luther King Jr. had invited Robinson to travel to Albany, Georgia, on August 26, 1962, to help rally a group of tired and beaten civil rights workers. The Albany campaign seemed to lack clear, and specific, objectives— which made victory difficult to achieve—and Robinson did the best he could to rally the troops. After delivering his speech, he then traveled to a church in Sasser, Georgia, that had been scorched because of its efforts to register African American voters. King later asked Robinson to chair a national committee that would raise funds to rebuild three burned churches, and Robinson agreed, eventually raising fifty thousand dollars for the campaign.
Source: New York Amsterdam News, September 22, 1962, 11.

HAVE YOU EVER attended the funeral of a church?

Not the funeral of a person at a church—the funeral of a church.

Just a few hours before writing this column, I stood before the smoldering ruins of what had once been the Mount Olivet Baptist Church in the backwoods community of Sasser, only a few minutes' drive out of Albany, Georgia.

I watched a strong man, the Rev. F. S. Swaggott, the pastor of the church, weeping as though his heart would break as he looked out over the debris and the wreckage of the institution into which he and his people had poured their devotion and their dreams.

Earlier in the day, I had had my eyes opened to what is really happening in Albany. You have to be there to really appreciate it. And when you come here, you've got to develop the greatest admiration and respect for these brave people. I remember the jam-packed audience where I delivered a speech. I encouraged people of Albany to carry on their magnificent fight and to cultivate the power of the ballot.

This way, they will be able one day to throw segregationists and race-haters out of the office and to elect decent men. It was a day of sweltering heat but that didn't keep Albany people and others of nearby communities from coming to listen, to pray and to sing. There must have been more than 1,000 persons outside the hall listening as the sound system carried our voices out to them.

I remember the faces of seven- and eight-year-olds as they sang with conviction the song that has become the theme of the Freedom Fighters of Albany.

"We shall overcome," they sang.

Standing there, in front of the smoking ruins, you think of how the news came through this same day, that another church, Mount Mary's at Chickasawhatchee, [had been burned]. That makes three churches murdered in recent months.

You remember what happened back in Albany earlier in the day. When someone suggested our coming to see the ruins, there was fear in the voice of someone who thought it might not be wise to go.

Your hosts, Dr. W. G. Anderson, youthful head of the Albany Movement and equally youthful Rev. Wyatt Tee Walker, Dr. Martin King's executive assistant, are men who do not know the meaning of fear. So you went out to the scene of the ruined church in three carloads.

There on the spot of that wreckage, you pledge a $100 contribution toward its rebuilding and the rebuilding of the other two Negro churches which have been leveled to the ground. These churches were desecrated simply because the leaders encouraged voter registration.

You know your own contribution is only a drop in the bucket. It will take about $25,000 to rebuild these churches. But they must be rebuilt and quickly. The Negro people must rebuild them to let the Klans and the Citizens Councils and the world know that we will not be frightened and will not allow our leaders to be intimidated.

I had no idea we would ever attempt to use this column in order to make a fund-raising plea. But I saw a picture in Albany and those surrounding communities which would leave me with a sense of guilt if I didn't try to do everything possible to let the Southern Negro know that I appreciate their devotion and sacrifice. I am, therefore, asking each and every reader who can do so to send a contribution and to solicit contributions from their friends.

We must not only rebuild these churches. We must also prepare to rebuild others. For the Klan and the Councils are not finished.

There will be more churches destroyed before this battle is over. If you will send your check to me, care of this newspaper, made out to The Southern Christian Leadership Conference, I will send it along to Dr. Martin Luther King Jr. at SCLC where it will be earmarked for the building fund of the organization.

Let's not let those kids down—the ones who sang: "We shall overcome."

Let's build proud, new, glorious, tall churches that will rise out of the ashes of hatred.

If I Were President

During his well-publicized trip to Africa in 1962, Democratic senator Allen El-lender of Louisiana, a thoroughgoing segregationist, stated that "the average African is incapable of leadership except through the assistance of Europeans."[5]
Source: *New York Amsterdam News*, December 29, 1962, 9.

---

5. "Travel Is So Narrowing," *Time*, December 14, 1962, 22.

IT'S ONLY ONE MAN'S OPINION, but there are two steps which I believe should be taken for the good of the country and in the interests of world peace.

If, by some tremendous miracle, I could become President of the United States for a few hours, I would do these two things.

I would sit down and write a personal letter to the chief of state of every African Government. The letter would go something like this:

"Dear Mr. Chief of State:

"As you are aware, there has been a great deal of publicity given to the fact that a United States Senator—Allen J. Ellender of Louisiana—has made statements which reflect his views that the African people are not ready for self-government.

"Senator Ellender, unfortunately, has been making 'so-called' 'fact-finding trips' for the Senate Appropriations Committee to inspect United States foreign operations abroad.

"I use the word 'unfortunately' because, while it is the prerogative of the Senate of this nation to designate its members for such assignments, I consider the Senator from Louisiana a disastrous choice for the task of conducting an objective investigation in Africa or Asia.

"Anyone, knowing the stand that Senator Ellender has taken with regard to people of color within his own nation, could have accurately predicted what his conclusions would be—even before he set out on his journey.

"As you are well aware, the Western powers have been bending every effort to persuade the people of the world that our way of life is superior to Communism.

"It is true that the State Department has already announced that Senator Ellender's observations do not reflect official policy.

"However, due to the fact that we who preach democracy must practice it more vigorously, if we are to be believed by the people of the world whose skins are dark, I thought that I should express to you my personal regrets concerning Senator Ellender's ill-chosen statements and my personal conviction that freedom is a thing for which man is innately 'ready' by virtue of birth."

The second thing I would do would be to call in my press secretary (I might even be a little cunning and call in my dark-skinned press secretary,

Andy Hatcher) and tell him to get the press boys together so I could personally read them the text of my letter.

I know that many Senators—Northern as well as Southern—would be angry with me.

I know I would catch the devil getting some of my legislative proposals through—which might make it harder for me to get reelected.

But I would take the position that there are times when it is more important to be a President than to be a politician.

"But, Jackie," I imagine someone is saying over my shoulder. "You are not the President and it isn't likely that you will be anytime soon."

Gosh, I can dream, can't I?

Jesse Owens Does Not Have It Made

Unlike Robinson, the star runner Jesse Owens, who had captured first place in the 200-meter dash at the 1936 Olympics in Berlin, was a conservative Republican who counted Booker T. Washington, with his focus on gradualism and individualism, as one of his heroes. Owens publicly opposed the confrontational tactics employed by Martin Luther King Jr., and in 1972 he wrote a book sharply critical of the Black Power movement.

Robinson refers in this column to boxing champion Floyd Patterson, who joined Jackie on a trip to support the Birmingham campaign led by King in 1963. Robinson could not have thought more highly of Patterson than he did—he found the boxer to be a gentleman, an athlete of the highest order, and, best of all, a committed advocate for civil rights.

Source: New York Amsterdam News, June 1, 1963, 11.

A FEW DAYS BACK, the wire services carried a statement reportedly made by Jesse Owens, who won lasting fame as an Olympic star and whose achievements were resented by Adolph Hitler. Jesse was quoted as saying he didn't see what good Floyd Patterson and I could achieve by making our trip to Birmingham at the height of the racial trouble brought about by demonstrations of the Negro people. He was further quoted as stating he had "never allowed himself" to become involved in such situations.

I was more than surprised that Jesse Owens could allow himself to be so quoted. I think it was perfectly clear to most people that Floyd and I went to Birmingham because we were invited there by Dr. Martin Luther King. We both felt that if Dr. King and those heroic marching kids could make the kind of sacrifices they made, the least that we in the North can do is to express our gratitude. Floyd and I wanted to let Dr. King and his followers know that we are on their side. We feel that any time the President of SCLC or any of the other civil rights leaders in the South think we can help, we owe it to ourselves and to them to do all we possibly can.

We have been criticized by pros. Yet no matter who says what, it does not change our determination to do the things and say the things we believe. While it may not please others for us to take certain stands, we are willing to face any of our critics so long as we are doing what we feel is right.

We could understand the New York *Daily News* writing an editorial agreeing with the Alabama editor who told President Kennedy that things would be fine in Birmingham if "outside agitators" like Patterson, Dr. King and I stayed away. The *Daily News*, in our opinion, has taken consistent stands against the best interests of minority people.

But we couldn't understand this kind of attitude expressed by one of our great athletes who ran into the same kind of bigotry in Berlin which is alive in Birmingham.

We wired Jesse in Chicago to ask if it was true that he had allowed himself to be used to express thoughts which could help the enemies of racial progress and true democracy. Jesse explained that he had not intended to knock what Floyd and I had done.

He admitted to a sincere fear that our trip might have inflamed the situation. I told Jesse that I hoped he realized how valuable it is to the segregationists to be able to quote a highly respected Negro who takes this kind of stand. What Floyd and I did was not very much to do—especially when you think of the real heroism of a Dick Gregory and an Al Hibbler, who truly let the Southern Negro know he does not stand alone.

Both Floyd and I are happy that we went to see Dr. King and to speak at mass rallies. It was one of the most moving experiences of our lives. Dr. King made us feel very humble in his attitude and statements that we had brought a little inspiration and encouragement to kids who braved the nightsticks, the police dogs—and now—dismissal from school—to help all of us.

We must keep these youngsters aware—and especially we who have been fortunate like Floyd, Jesse and myself—that no Negro has it made, regardless of his fame, position or money—until the most underprivileged Negro enjoys his rights as a free man.

When We're Divided

Martin Luther King Jr. and Jackie Robinson were heroes to each other, and both called upon the other to help their respective efforts in the civil rights movement. They also communicated with each other openly and frequently. In May 1960, for instance, Robinson penned King his concern that members of the Southern Christian Leadership Conference—which King had helped to found in 1957—were making disparaging remarks about the NAACP. "Let's not be a party to the old game of divide and conquer," Robinson wrote. "Talk like this sets our cause back."[6] Three years later, Robinson now makes the same point, this time to Roy Wilkins, who often criticized King and the SCLC over issues of fund-raising and tactics. Both Jackie and Rachel were very concerned about divisions within the civil rights movement and played the role of social hosts in bringing together the movement's leaders in informal settings where they could relax and engage in everyday conversations.
Source: New York Amsterdam News, July 6, 1963, 11.

I WAS SOMEWHAT DISAPPOINTED the other day when I read some statements the newspapers attributed to my friend, Mr. Roy Wilkins, the executive secretary of the National Association for the Advancement of Colored People.

6. Letter from Robinson to Martin Luther King Jr., May 5, 1960, MLKP-MBU, 600505-006. This number is the document identifier in the King Papers Project at Stanford University in California.

I am a member of the national board of the NAACP and I will tell anyone that Mr. Wilkins has done a magnificent job. Yet it shocked me the other day when he was quoted as casting disparaging remarks against other civil rights agencies.

Mr. Wilkins is alleged to have said that the NAACP does all the work and the other groups get all the publicity. He was quoted as appealing to people not to send their contributions to other groups, but to the NAACP.

Of course, the NAACP has done a grand job. And, of course, this organization needs and must have large sums of money in order to carry on. But I say to Mr. Wilkins that it is dangerously foolish for our own leaders to divide our ranks at a time when we need our greatest unity.

We cannot defend ourselves against those who would defeat our thrust toward human dignity if we are to fight within our own house and advertise the clash of our egos to the neighborhood.

I do not say this as a would-be leader. I do not think I have the ability and know I do not have the inclination for leadership. I say this as one man, one individual.

I say this as Robinson. If our leaders allow themselves to become involved in a power struggle—if they permit themselves to begin squabbling and pointing fingers at each other, we shall be lost.

If Malcolm Wants an All-Black Community, Why Doesn't He Just Go?

Although he was critical of Jesse Owens's nonconfrontational approach to social transformation, Robinson was no Malcolm X. Robinson's racial politics—with their firm opposition to both racial separatism and the use of any means necessary to accomplish racial justice—was much more in line with King's than with the politics embraced by Malcolm, the Nation of Islam minister and premier representative of black nationalism in the United States. Robinson refers below to Wyatt Walker, King's chief of staff; Ralph Abernathy, King's best friend and coleader in the movement; Fred Shuttlesworth, the famed civil rights leader based in Birmingham; George Lawrence, King's friend and minister of the Friendship Baptist Church in

New York City; and comedian Dick Gregory, another significant player in
the civil rights movement.
Source: New York Amsterdam News, July 13, 1963, 11.

MANY OF US were shocked to learn from our newspapers the other day
that Dr. Martin Luther King had been the victim of egg-throwing in
Harlem as he arrived at Salem Methodist Church to preach an evening
sermon.

The daily press attributed this disgraceful incident to the Black
Muslims.

Malcolm X, the leader of the Black Muslims, has denied that his organization had anything to do with the attack on Dr. King.

Assuming that Mr. X is telling the truth, we think that he must accept
some responsibility for helping to create a climate in the Harlem community which made it possible for such a despicable incident to occur.

It is reported that Malcolm called upon members of his group to turn
out and let Dr. King know what Muslims think of his nonviolent struggle
for integration. On any number of occasions, Malcolm has said for public
consumption that he is opposed to Dr. King's methods and philosophy.

Malcolm has just as much right to be opposed to Dr. King as anyone
else. Personally, I am not and don't know how I ever could be nonviolent.
If anyone punches me or otherwise physically assaults me, you can bet
your bottom dollar that I will try to give him back as good as he sent.

Yet I have to admire men like Dr. King, Wyatt Walker, Ralph Abernathy and Fred Shuttlesworth and all the rest who are loyal to the nonviolent discipline. I think it takes real guts for them to go through what they
endure and suffer.

Malcolm X and his organization believe in separation. They have
every right to. If they want to go off into some all-black community, why
don't they just go. I don't see how they can keep saying with a straight face
that their theories represent the will of the masses of the Negro people.

The masses of the Negro people, in cities all over the country, are
demonstrating, some at the risk of their lives, to give witness that they want
integration—the exact opposite of separation.

As I said, I feel the Muslims have a right to their opinions.

I do not think it is fair, however, for Malcolm to continue to make the kind of statements which incite people to attempt to dishonor a man of the integrity of Dr. King.

There is another angle to the anti-King demonstration. The Rev. George Lawrence, who drove Dr. King to the church and whose car was damaged during the incident, pointed out that had there been adequate police protection, the egg-throwing might have been prevented. Certainly the police know that Dr. King was once stabbed in Harlem. They should be furnishing him with every bit of protection he could possibly have. He gets it in Southern cities, why not in New York?

I must mention one other thing about the Muslims. As Dick Gregory has said, they've been in existence for thirty-five years, "but the Negro didn't know anything about them until the white man put them on his television." Gregory adds that Malcolm X has been invited to speak on white college campuses all over the nation, but seldom, if ever, gets invited to Negro college campuses.

It seems to me very odd that the power structure in journalism, television and radio keeps promoting the Muslims. The national Negro community has demonstrated dramatically that it is opposed to separation. Could it be that the Muslims are receiving important aid and sponsorship from outside the race?

Could it be that individuals or groups, which believe in segregation, find the Muslim version of segregation-separation useful to their cause? Where do the Muslims get their money? Who finances them? Does all their revenue come from membership? We think these are questions the Muslims ought to answer. We'd be delighted to have them do so.

How Deep Are the Wounds?

On April 23, 1951, sixteen-year-old Barbara Johns led her fellow students in a strike protesting inferior conditions at the segregated Robert Russa Moton High School in Farmville, Virginia. Because of overcrowding at the school, the local school board had constructed additional structures—tarpaper

shacks that lacked proper heating and water-resistant roofs. Frustrated by
the board's refusal to construct a new building in a timely manner, the stu-
dents walked out of school, and Johns appealed for help to NAACP attor-
neys who then filed a suit that eventually joined four other cases wrapped
together in the 1954 "Brown v. Board of Education" decision.
Source: New York Amsterdam News, January 18, 1964, 9.

THE OTHER DAY, the United States Supreme Court announced that
it will hand down a final decision after March hearings on the Prince
Edward County schools situation.

This will be a vital decision. Prince Edward County, in Virginia,
gained for itself the doubtful distinction of becoming the first county in
America to close down its public schools rather than obey the high court
integration edict.

As a result, Negro children of the county had been deprived of the
right to go to school for four years. . . .

Reading the news that our highest court is about to rule on this matter, we recalled having the pleasure of entertaining thirty of the Negro
students from Prince Edward. They had been brought East for a holiday
trip through the sponsorship of an enterprising interracial committee of
the Riverdale Community.

Both my wife and I were tremendously impressed with the manner
and dignity of these children who had been denied their right to an education because of the segregationists' determination to maintain the status quo.

The youngsters had a wonderful time. It was a sad thing, however, to
learn of an incident involving one of the visiting boys. He was the guest
of a Jewish family in Riverdale. One evening, during a discussion about
the Christian observance of Christmas, members of the host family told
him the story of Chanukah, the Jewish festival period which occurs close
to our Yuletide season.

This boy, we are told, became distressed and terribly angry. It had
come to him with great force that here was something he knew nothing
about and could not understand.

In the midst of real happiness over his visit here, he was oppressed with the feeling that he might never catch up with all he had lost during four years of his life when school doors had been slammed in his face because his face is dark.

What has America done to our children? How deep are the wounds which have been inflicted? Will they ever heal? How ironic that our legislators should be stalling on the civil rights issue.

Surely this nation can and must keep its promise—not only to its Negro citizens and youth—but to itself.

On May 25, 1964, the US Supreme Court ruled, in "Griffin v. County School Board of Prince Edward County," that federal courts could legally order the reopening of the public schools in the county.

Cassius Clay and His New Trainer—Malcolm X

Robinson was a huge fan of boxing in general and boxer Floyd Patterson in particular. Boxing great Sonny Liston had knocked out Patterson for the world championship title in 1962, and two years later a young Cassius Clay, much to Robinson's thrill, upset and dethroned Liston. During the weigh-in for the match, Clay had taunted Liston enough to earn a fine from the World Boxing Association. "I wanna rumble . . . I wanna rumble," Clay had chanted. "You're a tramp. I am going to eat you up. Somebody's going to die at the ringside tonight. Are you scared?"[7] Stylistically, Clay and Robinson were poles apart, but it seems that Robinson admired Clay's assertiveness in the public spotlight. Clay had changed his name to Muhammad Ali shortly before this column appeared, and it would take a while for Robinson to begin calling him by his new name.
Source: *New York Amsterdam News*, March 14, 1964, 13.

---

7. "1964: Cassius Clay Crowned World Champion," http://news.bbc.co.uk/onthis day/hi/dates/stories/february/25/newsid_4161000/4161687.stm.

IT WILL GO DOWN IN BOXING HISTORY how the myth of Sonny Liston, The Great Unconquerable, was exploded in the flurry of the hammering fists of a brash, brave and talkative young man.

Say all you will about Cassius and his great flow of language, his towering ego, his unorthodox manner of projecting himself. You must still admit that he put the deeds behind the words and came through victoriously.

Clay did more than win. He achieved the feat of outsmarting a man who had not only captured the title, but who had built a tremendous reputation for being able to scare his opponents, almost literally, to death. . . .

Many people have asked me if I am disturbed because, ideologically, Cassius has taken on a new trainer—Malcolm X. Why should I be disturbed? Clay has just as much right to ally himself with the Muslim religion as anyone else has to be a Protestant or a Catholic. There are those who scoff at the claim by Mr. Muhammad's Muslims that they represent a religion. These people have the right to their opinion. On the other hand, one of the basic American principles involves the right of each individual to embrace a philosophy and call it his religion.

People who are concerned over Clay's alliance with the Muslims seem mainly worried lest great flocks of young and adult Negroes will suddenly turn to the Islam ranks. I don't believe this will happen. I don't think the Negro people, en masse, will embrace Black Muslimism any more than they have embraced communism. Young and old, Negro people by the tens of thousands went into the streets in America and proved their willingness to suffer, fight and even die for freedom. These people want more democracy—not less. They want to be integrated into the mainstream of American life, not invited to live in some small cubicle of this land in splendid isolation. If Negroes ever turn to the Black Muslim movement, in any numbers, it will not be because of Cassius or even Minister Malcolm X. It will be because white America has refused to recognize the responsible leadership of the Negro people and to grant us the same rights that any other citizen enjoys in this land.

Despite the loudness—and sometimes crudeness—of Clay, he has brought excitement back into boxing. He has also spread the message that more of us need to know: "I am the greatest," he says. I am not advocating that Negroes think they are greater than anyone else. But I want them to know that they are just as great as other human beings. If we can learn to believe in ourselves one iota of the way Clay does, we'll be in great shape. I wish good luck to Cassius, but don't be surprised if Floyd Patterson becomes the first three-time champ one of these days.

The Counterrevolution of White People

On April 7, 1964, Governor George Wallace of Alabama, a fierce and outspoken opponent of Lyndon Johnson and civil rights legislation, captured 23 percent of the total vote in the presidential primary in Wisconsin. Robinson interpreted the vote as indicative of the white backlash moving across the country, and in the column below he denounces "white liberals" who seemed to have deserted the cause of civil rights when they could no longer define the movement's direction, policies, and speed. He also suggests a criticism that civil rights advocates often made—that many Americans were more concerned about the freedoms squelched by communists than they were about the absence of freedom for African Americans suffering the indignity of segregation and discrimination.

Source: New York Amsterdam News, April 25, 1964, 11.

UNDOUBTEDLY, MANY OF US are bitterly disappointed that, a Northern state like Wisconsin, home of so many second-generation Americans, could deliver to a segregationist like Governor Wallace almost a quarter of a million votes of confidence.

It merely goes to show, as Wisconsin's Governor has said, that there are many prejudiced people in that state. But the significance is deeper than this.

The Wisconsin vote was a fresh evidence of the white Northern counterrevolution which has been growing in resentment against civil rights legislation and the Negro demands for equality and justice.

The saddest part of it all is that this counterrevolution includes many so-called "white liberals" who were so horrified at the injustices committed in the South.

But when the barking dogs of Birmingham were stilled and the pressure of the fire hoses had been curtailed, the Negro in the North took a new and clear look at his own situation.

He found that segregation—and discrimination Northern-style, were as insidious as any open and frank Southern brutalities.

So the Negro in the North got on the march and the bleeding heart liberals suddenly realized that they didn't want job competition from the Negro.

They didn't want Negro children infiltrating their schools. They didn't want the Negro for a neighbor. They would much rather send a check to the NAACP, belong to some study group on race relations and observe Brotherhood Week one week out of the year.

This nation is in serious trouble. Too many of us fail to realize the depth of this trouble.

We are so certain of the strength of our democracy that those of us who really believe in it have become smug. We are concerned about the Castros and the Khrushchevs, the outsiders. We are not aware of the creeping corruption which threatens us from within.

One of the most dangerous threats is the symbolism represented in the candidacy of Senator Barry Goldwater. Many people, these days, are prone to dismiss Goldwater, to say his chances are declining, that he doesn't have a prayer to win the nomination of the Republican Party.

I am not so certain that the Goldwater threat is dead. I am certain that the impetus it was able to gain signifies great peril for democratic institutions. And I know that anything can happen in politics.

I realized that more keenly than ever on that ugly day of November 22, 1963, when a bright light went out in the city of Dallas.

If we want to preserve America—the America that was to be in the minds of its founding fathers—we had better wake up.

The counterrevolution of white people in America against the aims and aspirations of the Negro people in America is ugly.

It could lead to a counter-counterrevolution of the colored peoples of the world against the white peoples of the world. And the world's population is three-fourths colored people.

Be More than a Consumer

Jackie Robinson was far more favorable toward capitalism than Martin Luther King Jr. ever was. Whereas King steered toward democratic socialism, Robinson identified the creation of economic opportunity within capitalism as the best means for advancing civil rights. It is part of the reason that Robinson played a leading role in founding Freedom National Bank in Harlem at the end of 1964. He saw the new bank, whose board he initially chaired, as a way to help African Americans achieve economic independence from white financial institutions that often discriminated against them by denying them loans or setting interest rates artificially high.
Source: New York Amsterdam News, June 20, 1964, 11.

. . . [T]HERE IS STILL another consideration which is important to the welfare of the Negro: that is the need for him to become more integrated into the mainstream of our society's economy.

I am not speaking of job integration now. I am speaking of involvement in the world of business from the standpoint of becoming a producer, a manufacturer, a developer and creator of business, a provider of jobs. For much too long, the Negro has been only the consumer.

He has not taken advantage of the tremendous opportunities open to those who have the imagination to build small or large businesses and the courage to take a chance.

How much more effective our demands for integration in employment could be if we ourselves were providing an important number of job opportunities, not only for our own people, but also for others.

We must face the fact that we live in a very materialistic society. As a friend of mine likes to say, money doesn't only talk; it screams. Many of the social problems we have, many of the problems in the area of discrimination, are rooted in economic causes. I am not suggesting we should make ourselves slaves to money and worshipers of financial power.

Rather, we ourselves can enslave and use for our own purposes the productivity which financial accomplishment can bring.

Also, involving ourselves more firmly in the business world is bound to bring great benefits to our children. That is why I have become part of an insurance setup (a new and integrated one), a new bank and a public relations agency. I am tired of being just a consumer.

I hope that many of our young people will begin to think more in these terms. Security in a job is fine. So is the security you can build for yourself, if you believe in *you*.

Let's Not Cut Our Throats—Stay Away from Malcolm X

After leaving the Nation of Islam in March 1964, Malcolm embraced Sunni Islam, renounced his belief in racial separatism, and formed the Organization of Afro-American Unity as a way to establish connections between the civil rights movement in the United States and the wider liberation movement of oppressed people in developing countries.
Source: New York Amsterdam News, July 18, 1964, 21.

A RECENT EDITION of *The New York Journal-American* front-paged an article announcing the plan of ex-Black Muslim Malcolm X to "take over" the civil rights leadership. . . .

We would really be cutting our own throats if large numbers of our people listened to and followed the confused and confusing leadership which Malcolm projects.

Yesterday, he owed "all I am in life" to the Honorable Elijah Muhammad. Today the honorable Elijah is not so honorable in Malcolm's book. Yesterday, he vigorously denied that Muslims teach hatred. Today, he tells the white press that he became disenchanted with the Muslims because "they teach hate." Yesterday, to Malcolm all white folks were devils. Today, after seeing some startling vision during his travels, Mr. X has decided that some white folks are all right.

What does this man really think? What is he really after? How does he intend to spend the funds coming in from all those thousands of people he feels he can persuade to come up with a dollar a week? . . .

I shudder to think what would happen to our people and our country if some miracle placed a Malcolm X in command of our destiny. Of course, this will not happen. Perhaps some few thousands moved by Malcolm's bombastic eloquence, and by the fact that he is the fair-haired boy of the white press, will go along with him. I have too much faith in the commonsense of the majority of the Negroes to believe that Malcolm's new organization will ever amount to much.

Robinson did not publish a eulogy for Malcolm X at the time of his assassination, but Jackie remembered him fondly when struggling with the question of whether African American athletes should boycott the 1968 Olympics in Mexico City.

Robinson had "mixed emotions" about the proposed boycott. On the one hand, he knew that the international Games would be a wonderful platform for introducing African American athletes, and showcasing their talents, to US citizens and the wider world. On the other hand, he resonated with the black athletes' concerns about representing the United States abroad when the country still treated them like second-class citizens. "Maybe we as Negro athletes have 'been around' too long, accepting inequities and indignities and going along with the worn-out promises about how things are going to get better," Robinson wrote. "If this is the way the youngsters feel, believe me, I can sympathize with their point of view. Malcolm X, the late and brilliant leader, once pointed out to me during the course of a debate that: 'Jackie, in days to come, your son and my son will not be willing to settle for things we are willing to settle for.'"[8] That was quite a tribute to Malcolm X, and perhaps it demonstrated Robinson's increasing militancy in civil rights.

The proposed boycott never got off the ground; the organizers simply could not generate the critical mass of athletes that would be required to make a boycott successful and effective.

Three Beautiful Young Americans

During the summer of 1964—"Freedom Summer"—the Congress of Racial Equality (CORE) stepped up efforts to register African Americans to vote

8. *New York Amsterdam News*, December 16, 1967, 17.

in Mississippi. Three young civil rights activists working together on this effort—Michael Schwerner, James Chaney, and Andrew Goodman—visited Philadelphia, Mississippi, on the morning of June 21 to investigate the racially motivated torching of Zion Methodist Church. As they began to return to their home base in Meridian, they were arrested by the police and eventually lynched by members of the Ku Klux Klan, including members of the local sheriff's office. Robinson had been a longtime supporter of CORE—he was invited to become a board member in 1959—and was always crushed and angered when he learned of violence directed against children and youth. Robinson refers here to James Farmer, cofounder and national director of CORE.
Source: New York Amsterdam News, *August 22, 1964, 19.*

THE WORDS OF SORROW and anger have been uttered. The wrenching tears have blurred the eyes. The memorial tributes have been said. The dirge has been heard. The earth has been opened up to receive the tortured and brutalized bodies of three beautiful young Americans. The bell has tolled for Michael Schwerner, James Chaney and Andrew Goodman, who gave their lives in the belief that the corrupt state of Mississippi has a kinship with American democracy.

As Jim Farmer said, these three boys had "qualities which are more important in our world today than great wisdom or great power—qualities of gentleness, compassion and humanity."

It was a cruelly unnecessary twist to the story of these sadistic deaths that even in death there was discrimination. The goons who killed the two white boys and a Negro did such a horrible job on the Negro boy that Dr. David Spain, a Brooklyn pathologist who examined the bodies, made the following shocked statement about Chaney's remains:

"The jaw was shattered, the left shoulder and upper arm reduced to a pulp . . . the skull bones were broken and pushed in toward the brain. . . . In my extensive experience of 25 years as a pathologist, I have never witnessed bones so severely shattered except in tremendously high-speed accidents, such as plane crashes."

Not only were these three men classic prototypes of the new breed of valiant American youth which has been carrying on the struggle. They were also the sons of some truly fine American parents. These suffering, sorrowing people have let it be known that they intend to take up the torch for justice so nobly carried by their martyred boys.

At a time when persons of less stern stuff would be concentrating on their own grief, Rita Schwerner, the widow of Michael, is demonstrating the conviction of the families that life must proceed nobly. Jim Farmer, Paul Wilen (an architect) and I are co-chairing a drive to raise $25,000 for the creation of a new community center which will be built in Meridian. The Chaney-Goodman-Schwerner Center is to be a memorial to the three young men who were slain. . . .

In Defense of Martin Luther King, Jr.

Having arranged for the bugging of hotel rooms rented by Martin Luther King Jr., J. Edgar Hoover, the famous director of the Federal Bureau of Investigation, was privy to conversations that allegedly revealed sexual dalliances between King and women who were not his wife. Hoover simply detested King and no doubt had these tapes in mind when he publicly referred to King as "the most notorious liar in the country."[9] Hoover meant for his comments, as well as other FBI ploys, to force King to step down from his leadership in the civil rights movement. That disingenuous move did not work.

Source: New York Amsterdam News, December 5, 1964, 11.

THE VIOLENT AND VICIOUS ATTACK on Martin Luther King which came from the lips of J. Edgar Hoover gives one pause for deep reflection. For decades now, Mr. Hoover has been dealing with the most despicable murderers, kidnappers, rapists, gangsters and mentally, morally ill people imaginable.

To our knowledge, Mr. Hoover has always remained imperturbable, has never indulged in the name-calling business with regard to these social derelicts.

But now here comes the heroic chieftain of the Federal Bureau of Investigation, launching an ill-tempered and utterly stupid diatribe

9. Ben A. Franklins, "Hoover Assails Warren Findings," *NYT*, November 19, 1964, 1.

against a man who symbolizes the utmost in decency and courage in our society.

Mr. Hoover's absurd accusation that Dr. King is a "notorious liar" is evidence that the boss of the FBI is a much disturbed man. . . .

Mr. Hoover would appear to be feeling his years.

More importantly, there is something else the FBI boss seems to be feeling. Evidently, the truth hurts. And Dr. King did tell the truth—as other civil rights leaders have done—about the seeming inability of the FBI to take steps to protect American citizens of color in the South and to solve the many bombings of homes and churches.

Mr. Hoover may have the best of intentions but when you add up the score in failure to perform in the South, you have to wonder whether he has not come to an impasse in his ability to direct the chief law enforcement agency of our federal government. . . .

As one of our friends remarked, this latest anti-King blast will not hurt him. With Americans of decent indoctrination, Martin King needs no defense. If they don't know by now that he is the very characterization of integrity and courage, they will never know it.

Grownup Goons

A mob of white men wielding ax handles, pipes, and chains attacked African American schoolchildren on September 12, 1966, in response to the desegregation of public schools in Grenada, Mississippi. Several schoolchildren suffered broken limbs, bruised heads, and verbal abuse.

After throwing one young boy to the ground, a member of the mob shouted, "That'll teach you, nigger. Don't come back tomorrow."

"I don't want to come here anyway," the boy replied. "My mother sent me."

"You tell her if you come back here tomorrow," the adult thug spat back, "she'll be a dead nigger."[10]

Source: New York Amsterdam News, *October 1, 1966, 9.*

10. "Grenada Negroes Beaten at School," *NYT*, September 13, 1966, 1.

I GUESS WE, as Negro people, are really pretty naïve about this so-called Great Society in which we live.

We have witnessed some pretty raw brutalities—from the murder of Emmett Till and Medgar Evers—through the burning of churches and the execution of two white young men and a Negro in Philadelphia, Mississippi.

Somehow, however, like many of the Negro people I have talked with in recent days, we never did believe we would be reading newspaper accounts about a mob of sick sadists beating twelve- and thirteen-year-old school children. When this can happen in a community, that community has sunk into the very lowest depths.

I can just hear someone saying: "What did you expect? Remember the innocent Sunday School children cut down when the same type of maniac bombed a Birmingham church?"

The situation in Mississippi is discouraging enough. But when I think of that terrific and traitorous fight against the civil rights bill led by the aged Senator Everett Dirksen of Illinois, I really have to wonder where we are headed. In my opinion, the Illinois senator has earned the commission of commander-in-chief of the forces of white backlash.

Many of us believe that he is bowing to the panic which arose in the minds and hearts of many white people when they heard Stokely Carmichael's cry of "Black Power" echoing across the very state in which grown-up goons unmercifully whipped Negro kids who only wanted to go to school.

Some of the apologists for the legislators who failed to be true to their trust have brushed off the murder of the civil rights bill by pointing to the progress the Negro has been making. This is the stalest argument ever and I, personally, am sick of hearing it used as a cover-up. The Negro cannot be partially free any more than a woman can be partially pregnant. . . .

The Best of Black Power

Robinson had a complicated relationship with Adam Clayton Powell Jr., the colorful US congressman from Harlem. Although he appreciated Powell's contributions to the cause of civil rights through the years, as well as the community-based work he did for Harlem, Robinson found Powell to be

*egocentric, arrogant, and fonder of making headlines than of creating leg-
islation. In 1963 Robinson criticized Powell, in an open letter he published
in his column, for allegedly calling upon African Americans to boycott civil
rights organizations, like the NAACP, whose administrative and policy control rested at least partially in white hands.*

*Now, three years later, Robinson praises Powell for having publicly
denounced the definition of "Black Power" espoused by Stokely Carmichael,
a leader of the Student Nonviolent Coordinating Committee (SNCC). Carmichael had characterized Black Power as black separatism and the right
to bear arms—to use any means necessary in the fight for racial justice.
Conversely, Powell described Black Power as a form of black initiative and
responsibility, pride and productivity, and the belief that God created all of
humanity to live as a family.*

*Robinson's praise here does not represent a flip-flop in his assessment of
Powell. Rather, it simply shows Robinson's characteristic insistence on giving
credit where credit was due and criticism where criticism was due; he tended
not to allow past criticism or praise of a person to determine what he would
say about him or her at another point. In the following column, Robinson
also refers to other civil rights leaders, including labor leader A. Philip Randolph, the head of the Brotherhood of Sleeping Car Porters, whom Jackie
considered to be the elder statesman of the civil rights movement.*

Source: New York Amsterdam News, *October 22, 1966, 7.*

THE KIND OF LEADERSHIP which could help the black man to solve
his complex problems was verbalized recently from the pulpit of Abyssin-
ian Baptist Church. Adam Clayton Powell gave a magnificent interpre-
tation of "Black Power" and what it means to him. He issued a ringing
denunciation of the Stokely Carmichael version. The politico-minister's
words were indeed a blessing in this writer's opinion. . . .

I must admit that I like Dr. Powell's definition of "Black Power." Our
sincere faith and trust in God, a pride that has long been lacking among
most of us, black initiative (which at best could be found in a very small
percentage of our group), and black productivity obviously would move
us forward rapidly. Dr. Powell's call on his audience to "exercise a mass
responsibility for their fate" can be endorsed without hesitancy. While I

can't agree that our efforts in the past five years have been "a magnificent exercise of near futility with our marches, our picketing, and now our rebellion," I believe further use of these tactics would result in futility.

I believe had it not been for the massive marches, the courageous demonstrations and our heroic young people, our position would not today cause leaders to cast a worried eye. The president might not be pushing for civil rights laws or heads of state, city and local government seeking advice and guidance from qualified Negro leaders.

I suggest what is now needed is a sincere effort by Dr. Powell, Roy Wilkins, Dr. King, Whitney Young, and A. Philip Randolph to mobilize these forces and stop worrying about who is going to receive the credit. I believe the fault of our leaders is their drive for individual recognition with little or no concern about the results of an issue as long as personal attention is achieved. It's time we start praising when praise is due and damning when damning is due.

There is real strength among us. We are generally the balance of power in election, and earnings of 27 billion per year represent real strength. We have all kinds of definitions of black power. I salute Adam Powell for his latest version and suggest when we use our ballot and our dollars wisely, we are exercising black power without having to define it.

Robinson staked out a similar position in April 1967. When an interviewer asked him about Black Power, Robinson stated: "I don't advocate the Stokely Carmichael Black Power situation, because it can only get us in trouble. But if we're talking about the wise use of political strength, then I say we ought to have Black Power. But if we're talking about getting in the streets, resorting to violence, creating disturbances, this cannot help anything. Black Power in this sense is just as bad as white power in that sense, so I'm opposed to it." Robinson also stated in the interview that Carmichael's version of Black Power would be counterproductive exactly because it would "only get us more [Alabama governor George] Wallaces elected to office."[11]

11. Transcript of interview with Theodore Granik, "Youth Wants to Know," April 1967, Jackie Robinson Papers (JRP), box 9, Library of Congress, Washington, DC.

Wilkins, Make Way for the Young Turks!

Robinson was a longtime supporter of the NAACP. He had won the Spin-garn Medal, the organization's annual award for distinguished achieve-ment, in 1956; helped to direct its Freedom Fund campaign for several years; and then served for many years as a board member. But here he directs very pointed criticism at Roy Wilkins, the NAACP executive secretary, who was known for bristling at any critical remarks that came his way. Robinson would later praise Wilkins for opposing the black nationalism of militant members of the National Black Political Convention held in 1972.
Source: New York Amsterdam News, *January 14, 1967, 13.*

THIS IS A COLUMN I have often considered doing—and one I wish I didn't have to write. I have to write it because I do not buy the philosophy that being a Negro takes away one's right to criticize another Negro. I don't believe we reach maturity as a people until we can engage in the constructive give and take of honest criticism.

So here goes! As a former national board member of the NAACP, as a longtime admirer of the organization, as one who has traveled thousands of miles and helped raise hundreds of thousands of dollars for the orga-nization, I am forced to say sadly that I am terribly disappointed in the NAACP and deeply concerned about its future.

This disappointment and concern are not new to me. They are feel-ings which have been growing over the years. I have watched the stran-gling political grip which Roy Wilkins and a clique of the Old Guard of the NAACP have held over the ruling board of directors.

I have watched the brave but unsuccessful efforts of younger, more vibrant, more aggressive, well-prepared insurgents to inject new blood and new life into the association. But Mr. Wilkins and his Old Guard always seem to manage to stomp these efforts down.

Realistically, we recognize that the NAACP is so structured that an executive secretary who cannot exercise control is a fool of the first order.

Over the Wilkins years, however, it is my humble opinion and that of many people I have talked with, that the National Office has been run as a kind of dictatorship insensitive to the trends of our times, unresponsive to the needs and aims of the Negro masses, especially the young, and more and more seeming to reflect a refined: "Yessir, Mr. Charlie" point of view.

This determination to keep things as they have been instead of the way they ought to be may be gaining Ford Foundation money, but it is not gaining respect of the younger people of our race, many of whom feel the NAACP is archaic and who reject its rigid posture completely.

I had become so frustrated with what I had come to see as the rapid decline of the organization that I requested that my name not be offered for reelection to the board.

Maybe I should have stayed in the fight to try to help save our oldest civil rights agency from an infantile kind of paralysis.

Wilkins replied to Robinson with a detailed letter of defense that concluded with a pot shot: "One of these days before you are seventy, some down-to-earth wisdom will find its way into your life. If it does nothing except stop you from believing that 'because I see it this way I have to say it,' it will have done a great service."[12]

Dirty Spics?—No!

Robinson refused to see the civil rights movement as primarily, or solely, about African Americans, and here he draws a close connection between African Americans, Hispanics, and Jews—a connection that some civil rights leaders chose not to make.
Source: New York Amsterdam News, January 28, 1967, 15.

I ONCE READ—and have long remembered—a very simple story of how one Negro man rejected the words of a bigot.

Riding in a taxicab, this man was drawn into a conversation with the very talkative driver. Things went well until . . . a youngster scooting across

12. Letter from Roy Wilkins to Robinson, February 8, 1967, JRP, box 4, folder 23.

the street in Spanish Harlem—a Puerto Rican—narrowly missed being hit by the cab.

Upset, the white driver fussed and fumed. "The dirty spics," he said. "Why do they let them come here and mess up our neighborhoods and take over our jobs?"

"Spics, huh?" the Negro passenger responded. Then he asked: "What have you got in your other pocket for niggers?"

The cabdriver was floored, but he quickly got the message. He knew his passenger was a man who resented all kinds of bigotry. Nine chances out of ten, when a person will speak disparagingly of a Jew or Puerto Rican, you can bet he'll handle you the same way the instant you turn your back.

It is the duty and responsibility of each and every one of us to refuse to accept the faintest sign or token of prejudice. It does not matter whether it is directed against us or against others. Racial prejudice is not only a vicious disease, it is also contagious.

4

On Peace with Justice

The Time for Excuses Has Long Passed

On April 25, 1959, a mob of whites kidnapped Mack Charles Parker from his cell in the Pearl River County, Mississippi, courthouse, where he had been waiting for his trial on charges of raping a white woman, and riddled his body with bullets before dumping it into the Pearl River. A month later, the federal government claimed that no federal crime had been committed in the lynching and withdrew from the case, turning over evidence gathered by the FBI to J. P. Coleman, the governor of Mississippi.
Source: New York Post, May 29, 1959, 72.

SO IT'S THE SAME OLD STORY all over again. A Negro is boldly and brutally lynched in Mississippi. The murderers are reportedly known and identified. And yet everybody claims there's nothing whatsoever that can be done about it.

I said in this space a few weeks ago that I was confident the FBI would turn up the evidence to solve this outrage. And apparently they have. But now, despite all the brave statements a month ago that the federal government would do all in its power to bring the lynchers to justice, despite reports that the president had taken a personal interest in the case—despite all this, the Justice Dept. has decided to throw in the towel and, wonder of wonders, turn over to the Mississippi officials themselves the evidence they have gathered.

I've read all the comments and legal justifications for all of this, but I don't mind admitting that I'm tired of hearing excuses. I just can't understand for the life of me how we in America can allow this kind of thing to happen, and then just sit by helplessly and do nothing about it.

All over the world today the news is being read, broadcast and discussed. America is struggling as never before for the goodwill and alliance of the uncommitted peoples of the world. And yet, without firing a single shot, our enemies today can merely point to the headlines in our own newspapers and say, "See there? That's what America thinks of people whose skin color is not 'right.' How can you trust a country that says one thing in the UN—and refuses to clean up its own back yard?"

I'll be quite frank here and say that I am angry. And I think people all over the country—Negro and white—are angry, too, and have a perfect right to be. We don't like being left out on a limb, and we don't like being deceived. And that's just what I think has happened in this case.

I'll be frank again. I think our government officials, from President Eisenhower on down, should know that we have been waiting patiently for people's hearts to change. It's been about 96 years at last count since the Emancipation Proclamation. But from reports I've been receiving lately, if the federal government doesn't recognize its responsibility to implement the equal-justice-under-law provisions of our Constitution and prevent such open outrages as this, then I'm concerned that sentiment may grow that Negroes will have to defend themselves.

And this is just what I'm afraid of. Let me say right here and now that no one should counsel violence, or fighting fire with fire, or any of the other calls to other than legal, peaceful means. I can't emphasize too strongly how tragic it would be for Negroes—or whites, either for that matter—to try to solve these problems by hate, violence and spite, no matter how provoked anyone may feel.

So I'm greatly concerned when I open mail from Negro people in the South, or talk with them in person and hear them say, as one man recently told me: "They taught me how to defend myself in the Marine Corps. And the next time the Klan rides in my town, I'd be a fool if I didn't shoot back."

Or this in a recent letter from a rising young leader: "Nonviolence may win a seat on a bus, but it won't stop an angry mob."

And one of the reasons I'm so concerned is that I clearly recognize these fellows are merely beginning now to say publicly what numbers of

Negroes have been saying privately for some time. Whole communities in the South are actually sitting on the verge of eruption, as people tell me privately day after day. And on top of this explosive situation comes fuel for the fire: a helpless Negro prisoner is lynched and the federal government washes its hand and tells Mississippi it will have to handle the case itself.

It goes without saying that the governor of Mississippi can hardly be expected to do a single blessed thing with the evidence turned over to him. In fact, on the day it was revealed the FBI had actually named names and detailed actions, Gov. Coleman was on his way to Washington to testify against new civil rights legislation. And he did so testify yesterday.

I've already said that I don't label myself as any official spokesman for other Negroes. But for what it's worth, I appeal to Congress, to the Justice Dept. and to President Eisenhower to take steps now to remedy this miscarriage of justice. If it's new legislation that's needed, then let's have it. If it's more vigorous use of already existing laws, then let's get to it without further delay. And if it's new officials we need to really sign in and do a job, then let there be no hesitation.

The time for excuses and apologies is past. Negroes can't afford this, whites can't afford it, and America can't afford it. The federal government must act now.

A grand jury in Mississippi adjourned in November 1959 without acting on the Parker case, or even calling FBI witnesses who had gathered evidence. There were no convictions.

Violent Intimidation Continues

Robinson frequently drew public attention to the threats made against Martin Luther King Jr. and other civil rights leaders. Three years after writing the prophetic column below, and in the wake of the assassination of NAACP field secretary Medgar Evers in Mississippi, Robinson even lobbied the White House to provide King with greater protection.
    Source: New York Post, February 26, 1960, 80.

IN THE WAKE of the student demonstrations against lunch-counter seg-regation which are sweeping the South, it is not at all surprising that the leading American proponent of nonviolent direct action has again been arrested on a hastily framed charge.

The Rev. Martin Luther King, Jr., hero of the successful Montgomery, Ala., bus boycott had just returned from consulting with student leaders in North Carolina when he was indicted by Alabama for alleged perjury in filing state income tax returns.

The State of Alabama has tried several times before to "get" Rev. King. He has been arrested some seven times in the last four years, for every-thing from minor traffic "violations" to leading an "illegal" boycott of segregated buses. Attempts have been made to buy him off, to intimidate him through constant police harassment, and even to murder him and his family by bombing his home in the middle of the night. And now that he has moved the base of his operations from Montgomery to Atlanta, Ala-bama has been reduced to using its legal machinery—which is firmly in segregationist hands—to try to get him on a false issue. . . .

. . . But King's arrest and indictment seem to me indicative of a serious and alarming attempt to discredit and eliminate militant Negro leader-ship in an effort to slow down the already minute pace of recent advance. There have been many other instances.

Florida NAACP leader Harry T. Moore and his wife were unmerci-fully shot to death through the window of their home on Christmas night 1951. Mississippi NAACP leader Rev. George W. Lee was murdered for daring to attempt to register for voting in Belzoni, Miss., in 1955. Gus Courts, who succeeded him, was filled with buckshot in his grocery store for refusing to take his name off the voting lists. And Lamar Smith was murdered in broad daylight on the steps of the courthouse in Brookhaven, Miss., in 1955. Needless to say, no one has ever been apprehended for a single one of these crimes.

I could go on: the Rev. J. A. Delaine, who helped initiate the original South Carolina suit which resulted in the 1954 Supreme Court school desegregation decision, escaped with his life only by firing back at his attackers from his parsonage window after his church had been burned to the ground. Mrs. Daisy Bates's newspaper, the Arkansas *State Press*, was forced out of business by Faubus and his followers. Her home has been repeatedly attacked, and even the home of one of the Little Rock students was bombed early this month. In Birmingham, the Rev. F. L. Shuttlesworth daily faces the same kind of harassment that Rev. King has borne.

The question is: whom will they try to get now? Will it be Roy Wilkins or A. Philip Randolph? Thurgood Marshall or the leaders of the student protest? It might easily be any or all of these once they dispose of their Number One target, Martin Luther King. . . .

If Rev. King is allowed to be picked off, it will strengthen the resolution of the segregationists to deprive Negroes of effective leadership. Though he has often expressed his willingness to pay with his life, if need be, to help secure the course of decency and justice, it is all too clear that not just Negroes but all America desperately needs the wise leadership of men like Martin Luther King.

The Right to Hate

Twenty-two years before Robinson published this column, NAACP attorney Thurgood Marshall kept close watch over the special investigative committee that would become known as the House Un-American Activities Committee. In its early form, HUAC—which turned its sights on communists, Nazis, fascists, and anything resembling un-Americanism—was known as the Dies Committee because its cochairman was Representative Martin Dies Jr. of Texas, a prosegregationist. And in September 1940, Marshall wrote Dies a letter asking him to investigate the Ku Klux Klan rather than the organization that the congressman had his eyes on—the NAACP.

Interestingly, Robinson himself appeared before HUAC on July 18, 1949, at one of its hearings on African American loyalty in the United States. In his widely publicized testimony, Robinson criticized Paul Robeson, the internationally renowned singer and actor, for having questioned whether African Americans, long denied fundamental rights, would fight for the United States in a war against the Soviet Union, a country that had a far better record on civil rights.

Source: *New York Amsterdam News*, August 25, 1962, 11.

MOST PEOPLE dislike to admit it. However, it is a fact that individuals have the legal right to hate other individuals.

It is also a fact that there is no manmade law designed to force people to love one another.

Of course, there is a law of ethics, morality and of religious conscience which says that hate is wrong and love is right.

Pennsylvania Democrat Representative Francis E. Walter seems to be one of those who doesn't realize that a black man has as much right to hate a white man as a white man has to hate a Negro.

Congressman Walter has announced that his House Un-American Activities Committee is considering launching "a very intensive investigation of a Negro group known as the Black Muslims."

We didn't hear a mumbling word from Mr. Walter during all those years when members of the White Citizens Councils—those folks who don't wear sheets—were spreading poison propaganda against Negro people in the South.

Mr. Walter had nothing to say when the Ku Klux Klan—folks who do wear sheets—was intimidating, threatening, kidnapping, beating, maiming and even killing Negroes whenever a lynching atmosphere could be created.

Isn't it a little strange that Mr. Walter's passion for investigation wasn't aroused when it became obvious that Negro Americans were being denied their constitutional rights by the little band of men who run a town called Albany, Georgia?

This writer makes no brief for the preachments of the Black Muslims. Personally, I could never become a Black Muslim follower if for no other reason than my opposition to the advocacy of black supremacy. I cannot repeat too often that I consider black supremacy as dangerous as white supremacy.

Furthermore, I believe integration will be the answer to the problem of Americans of both races. The Muslims believe in separation and ask that they be given a state to which Negro people may go and have their own society.

In spite of my personal differences with the Black Muslims, I believe they have as much right to hate the white man—if it is true that they do— as any white man has the right, legally, to hate the black man.

Personally, it makes no difference to me if someone hates us. It is only when he begins putting his foot on our neck, keeping us from getting a job, walking in a public park, taking a book out of a public library, voting at the polls, living in a neighborhood we can afford—it is only then that I will holler loud and long.

Many charges have been made against the Muslims. But few have been proven. Whenever one of the many splinter groups of black nationalists becomes embroiled in an explosive situation, it is usually blamed on the Black Muslims.

Congressman Walter's decision to consider probing this group was made after his fellow Democrat, Rep. Mendel Rivers of South Carolina, had charged that the Black Muslims are "dedicated to murder, naked violence, hatred, mugging and yoking."

One of the fortunate things about being a congressman is that you have the right to make all sorts of wild, unsubstantiated charges on the floor of Congress without having to prove them or running the risk of getting sued.

Certainly, no one has ever proven that the Black Muslims have perpetrated anything like the terrible deeds openly and boldly committed by the Klan or by Gestapo Southern police officers who beat pregnant women and bloody the heads of Negro attorneys.

Congressman Walter does a disservice to his own political party, which claims to be so much on the side of the Negro, when he has a blind spot for wrongs perpetrated against the Negro and such enthusiasm about investigating the Black Muslims. . . .

Heart to Heart about Violence

Approximately seventy-five African American children and youth were involved in vandalism at a fruit and vegetable stand in Harlem on April 17, 1964. The relatively minor event exploded into what became known as the Fruit Riot when police used brutal tactics against the vandals. In the weeks following the riot, an antiwhite gang known as the Blood Brothers undertook heavy recruiting and then trained the young recruits in karate and other means of defense. At the same time, racially motivated violence against whites seemed to be increasing markedly.

Source: New York Amsterdam News, June 13, 1964, 21.

WITHIN THE PAST FEW WEEKS, acts of violence and vandalism on the part of Negro youngsters in Harlem and Brooklyn have commanded the headlines of the daily press. . . .

I wish I could have a heart-to-heart, man-to-man talk with some of the youngsters who, by their blindly reckless acts, are endangering the freedom struggle. I would tell them that they are playing right into the hands of the enemy.

I would tell them that they are alienating from our cause people of goodwill who could bring something of value to our search for freedom. I would say to them frankly that no one who is sincere about freedom will desert the fight because of isolated instances which are exaggerated in the press.

But I would point out to them that, whether or not anyone is justified in deserting the cause for this spurious reason, the fact is that this is what is happening. I would say to them that, first and foremost, they are doing themselves great harm, destroying their own lives and injuring their own personalities.

I would say next that they are hurting the image of the community in which they live. I would remind them that they are bringing grief to their families and friends. I would add that they are violating the basic principle of the good life by striking out at people who are, in the main, innocent people.

I would tell these kids that they are hurting our chances of winning the greatest goal which a people have ever sought to attain. I would point out to them that they are stomping brutally on the graves of the Birmingham kids, on the soil beneath which a Medgar Evers and a John Kennedy sleep the sleep of martyrdom. I would say to them that they are building the links in a chain which could hold their children to come and their children's children in the grip of the same slavery of segregation from which we now seek to break loose.

I do not believe there is any organized hate movement among the Negro people. That is one lesson, thank God, that we have failed to imitate despite the example set for us by the white man. I do know that there are resentments and despairs and fears and frustrations which drive some of these youngsters to lash out and seek freedom.

But I would say to them, man to man, that you don't win like this. You don't free yourselves or your brothers of color like this. I would say there is a better way and, frankly, I don't happen to be one of the turn-the-other-cheek advocates, despite my deep admiration for Dr. Martin King. Personally, I am afraid I have not learned to return hatred with love.

But neither do I believe that the road to progress lies along the twisted route of degenerate and immoral behavior. That's what I would like to say to the kids who are helping to make the headlines which make an entire city shudder.

I Am Not Nonviolent, but Wiser NAACP Youth Are

Robinson never fully developed a personal theory about the justifiability of using force, but it is unmistakably clear that he favored the use of controlled force under certain circumstances. Unlike his friend Martin Luther King Jr., Robinson often noted that a commitment to nonviolence did not seem to be part of his moral character.

Nevertheless, he fully supported the nonviolent tactics that King adopted in all of his campaigns and sharply criticized black militants who advocated the use of any means necessary, including force, to advance the cause of civil rights.

Source: New York Amsterdam News, July 11, 1964, 19.

. . . I GOT A DRAMATIC, firsthand lesson in the wonderful way our civil rights youth of both races conduct themselves the other day when I was a guest of honor at an NAACP youth banquet held in Washington during the NAACP's 55th annual convention. . . .

The banquet was proceeding according to plan when, to the astonishment of all of us, a white man leaped up on the dais and began shouting some words about "sending all the niggers back to Africa."

The man was waving a swastika and was evidently part of a swastika-wearing group which had been picketing in front of the hotel when the guests arrived for the banquet.

I will be very honest with you. I am not nonviolent in such circumstances. I felt my anger rising within me at the thought of some racist trying to create confusion at a time when serious, sober young people were carrying out what they believe to be their duty as young citizens and patriots.

Not only was my anger rising, but I found that I was rising with every intention of letting this unexpected visitor have a good swift jab in the head. Luckily, the NAACP youngsters were quicker than I was. They got to him first. They didn't hit him.

They didn't maul him. They surrounded him, took hold of him and hustled him out of the room.

They were determined but calm. I had to admit that they were showing a greater wisdom about the incident than I had been able to display.

I couldn't help thinking what would have happened to some Negro if he had had the temerity to intrude on a white-dominated function in such an outrageous manner.

Typical of the mentality of the self-styled American Nazis, in the confusion created by the intruder, a confederate of his released some mice which scurried about the room, causing confusion and dismay among the dining guests.

It was a mean, nasty thing to do and it made me realize that there are some two-legged, grownup mice—rats, I mean, of course—in the world.

Those kids, however, have something more than just courage and poise and dignity. They also have the wonderful quality of humor. Noting that the unwelcome mice were of different colors, one of the youngsters was heard to remark:

"Well, at least they are integrated."

I think the future of America is in good hands as long as we have fine young people like this who know what they want, who have the courage to go after it and the great depth of soul to carry themselves in a manner which can only make appreciative people proud.

Julian Bond Has the Right to Be Wrong

Robinson offers a vigorous defense of civil rights activist Julian Bond, a former director of communications for the Student Nonviolent Coordinating Committee. Bond was an outspoken critic of the Vietnam War during his race for a seat in the Georgia state legislature—a role that did not sit so well with the state's conservative politicians. Bond would later chair the NAACP board for many years.

Source: New York Amsterdam News, *January 29, 1966, 15.*

SEVERAL YEARS AGO, a young, articulate and intelligent young Negro was ejected from the then "for white only" visitors section of the Georgia state legislature.

Several weeks ago, this same young man walked proudly back into the chambers where Georgia's legislators meet.

This time, he walked into those chambers armed with the votes of black people who had chosen him to represent them.

He was thrown out again—only this time, not physically. The legislature refused to seat him. Their reason—that he had expressed sentiments disagreeing with the nation's war policy in Vietnam.

If I have read accurate reports of what Julian Bond has said about our foreign policy, I strongly disagree with him. I have a boy in Vietnam and, with my son, Jackie, Jr., I believe it is our duty, as much as anyone else's, to support the president and our Congress in its decisions on foreign policy.

However, one of the things we are fighting for, I deeply hope, is the right for men to have freedom of opinion, freedom of thought and freedom of speech.

Julian Bond ought to have that right.

He is denied it when a bunch of reactionary segregationists take it upon themselves to bar him because he voiced his beliefs. The Georgia legislature strikes the phony moral pose that Mr. Bond is an enemy of the Constitution. How about all those Southern bigots who defied Supreme Court decisions, who flouted the legislative, judicial and moral laws in order to preserve the status quo and keep the Negro "in his place."

The charge against Bond is a cynical and cruel mockery of everything we consider to be pure democracy and simple justice. Every citizen who believes in these principles should write to his congressman to ask that pressure be brought to bear on the governor and the legislature of Georgia.

If we are to live in a nation which denies its own citizens the right to dissent, we shall be living in a nation on its way downhill to second class status in this changing world.

Martin Luther King Jr. Is Still My Leader

On April 4, 1967, Martin Luther King Jr. stood in the esteemed pulpit of Riverside Church in New York City and delivered his most famous speech on the Vietnam War. His condemnation of the war evoked criticism from virtually all quarters, from conservative politicians to the editorial board of the "New York Times" and numerous leaders within the civil rights movement. Robinson offered his own critical reaction in a May 13 column that he used for an "open letter" to King. On the one hand, Robinson stated that King should recognize that his proposed cease-fire would give the Vietcong an opportunity to gain more resources for killing more US troops. On the other, he wrote that King unfairly focused on mistakes made by the United States, in effect giving the Vietcong a moral pass. Robinson concluded the open letter by inviting King to offer a response. The civil rights leader did respond—with a phone call—and the following is Robinson's glowing account of both the historic call and his reaction to it.
Source: New York Amsterdam News, July 1, 1967, 17.

THE TELEPHONE RANG.

Before the rich, deep voice identified the caller, I knew that he was my dear friend, Dr. Martin Luther King, Jr.

He was calling with regard to the open letter which I wrote him in this column—a letter expressing my confusion and distress over his stand on Vietnam. I had invited him to prepare a reply which I would have been happy to publish. Characteristic of Martin, he did not rush to accept this offer simply to justify himself in the eyes of those who had read my open letter.

He is a man who is not defeated by criticism, particularly when he is speaking from conviction. I believe that he speaks from conviction one hundred percent of the time. The reason he was calling me was that he was concerned that I, as a friend, understand his philosophy and his motivation.

We had a long—and for me—a most enlightening conversation.

I had understood that, as a man of God, Martin had been compelled from within to speak out against war and for peace.

I understood that, as a leader who is not merely a civil rights leader, he would have been untrue to himself had he not taken a stand for a principle in which he so deeply believed.

I understood that, as a Nobel Peace Prize winner, it was logical that he have as much concern for waging peace as some people have for waging war.

I realized that the Martin King who suffered and risked life for nonviolence in Montgomery, in Birmingham, in Selma—and yes, in the North—that same Martin King is the man who now cries out for nonviolence in Vietnam.

All these things I had understood.

I understood also how Martin felt as a father whose daughter once said to her mother, "Mommy, I don't want to be blown up." I understood how he felt as the husband of a wonderful woman who, for many years, unheralded, has been working in the world peace movement.

But there were other things I did not understand. Was he really advocating a marriage of the civil rights and peace movements—and, if so, would such a marriage be a disastrous alliance? Why did he seem to confine his criticism to the deeds of the U.S. and to ignore the deeds of the Viet Cong? What was the background of his knowledge to assess the war situation? Was he really convinced that the president is not doing all in his power to bring the war to a halt?

These—and other questions—we discussed. I would be foolish to attempt to give you, secondhand, the brilliant arguments he advanced.

I have not given up the hope that he will—in spite of that backbreaking schedule of his—find time to do a guest column or two in this space—to express them himself.

But there is one central point I want to make. It is a truth which my friend Martin King understands absolutely. And I want to make sure that you do.

I am no hypocrite. So I will not say that I have changed all the opinions I had which seemed to differ from what I understood to be Dr. King's opinions. But I am proud to say that this man is, in my opinion, the finest leader the Negro people have and one of the most magnificent leaders the world has today. I respect him because, no matter how I may disagree with him, I know that he is a sincere man. I know that he has the capacity to make the hard decision of saying precisely what he thinks, whether it is a popular thing to say or not.

He is still my leader—a man to whose defense I would come at any time he might need me. That is a personal commitment and a public pledge.

So I had to write this column because I would not want bigots and those who secretly hate Dr. King to find comfort in my disagreeing with him. Let there be no doubt in any man's mind where I stand on the subject of Dr. Martin Luther King, Jr. If ever a man was placed on this earth by divine force to help solve the doubts and ease the hurts and dispel the fears of mortal man, I believe that man is Dr. King.

Why Riots Happen

Conservative commentators saw the Watts riots—as well as other riots exploding throughout urban areas at this point—as the result of poorly formed moral character. But Robinson pinpoints a different cause in this column.

A week before Robinson published this column, H. Rap Brown, the new chairman of the Student Nonviolent Coordinating Committee, made an appearance in Robinson's old neighborhood in St. Albans, Queens, telling a crowd of fifteen hundred supporters that recent race riots were "dress rehearsals for revolution."[1] Brown also called upon his supporters to attend a hearing at Queens County Criminal Court in a show of support for seventeen African Americans, some of them members of the Revolutionary Action Movement (RAM), who had been indicted for plotting to murder Roy Wilkins of the NAACP and Whitney Young of the Urban League, two leaders whom militants characterized as far too moderate for advancing the cause of justice for African Americans. Robinson found Brown to be a sensationalist, dangerous, irresponsible agitator with a talent for igniting fires and then getting himself safely out of the way, leaving the people he agitated to face the flames.

Source: New York Amsterdam News, August 12, 1967, 17.

. . . RIOTS DO NOT HAPPEN because a cop strikes a boy or a teenager resists arrest or because a crowd seeks to restrain an officer from making an arrest.

Riots begin with the hopelessness which lives in the hearts of a people who from childhood expect to live in a rundown house, to be raised by one parent, to be denied proper recreation, to attend an inferior school, to experience police brutality, to be turned down when seeking a decent job and to watch the spectacle of a Senate bigot baiting one of the most brilliant black men of our society. . . .

The Only Way I Know How to Be Me

Robinson was no stranger to death threats. While playing for the Dodgers, he had received more than a few notes from individuals claiming that they would shoot him if he attempted to play ball in their hometown. And when he challenged black militants in Harlem in the early 1960s, more vicious death threats came his way. In the column that follows, Robinson describes a particular threat he received in the mail. His use of "Ram" refers to the

1. Homer Bigart, "Rap Brown Calls Riots 'Rehearsals for Revolution,'" *New York Times*, August 7, 1967, 1.

Revolutionary Action Movement, the black paramilitary group whose leaders, as noted above, were arrested in June 1967 for allegedly plotting to kill Roy Wilkins of the NAACP and Whitney Young of the National Urban League. RAM's plan was to foment an uprising of blacks, especially young black militants, by killing the civil rights leaders and then blaming the deaths on whites.

Source: New York Amsterdam News, October 7, 1967, 15.

THE DAILY PRESS has a habit of labeling the louder, more rabble-rousing and more sensation-minded Negroes "militants." I suggest some of the editors look the word up because, as they employ it, it is definitely a misnomer. Dr. Martin Luther King, Jr., recently told a newsman that he supposed what the newsman meant, in referring to some other leaders, was that they were "military" rather than militant. Dr. King has clear title to this observation. For, nonviolent though he may be, Martin King is one of the most militant men in the world.

I think it is high time that more of our middle-class Negroes drop their "above the battle" role and become involved with the struggles of our masses. We are allowing people who speak for a few and who do not project ideas and philosophy not shared by the majority to take the stage and dominate the spotlight. I believe there are many of us of the middle class who can be as militant in the cause of our people as anyone else. I consider it my duty to be so.

The Good Lord has showered blessings on me, and this country, and its people, white and black, have been good to me. I have been very fortunate and I realize that I do not have the same problems as the masses of our people. But no matter how rich or famous I might become, no matter what luxuries or special privileges I might achieve, no matter how many powerful friends I might make, I would never be the man I want to be until my humblest brother, black and white, becomes the man he wants to be.

So I must be involved in our fight for freedom. I'd like to see many other middle-class Negroes become so involved. It is not a simple or easy step. It might even be a dangerous one in view of the lunatics and fanatics lurking on the sidelines.

I have been writing and speaking out against violence, about separate black societies and about certain interpretations of Black Power with which I do not agree.

My mail has become enlivened with some pretty nasty letters—even some threats. Not too long ago I received in the mail a card from a deck of playing cards—the black ace of spades. The word "Ram" was inscribed on the card. I don't know whether it was the real thing from that group which drew a lot of publicity and the arrest of some of its members in an alleged plot to kill Roy Wilkins, Whitney Young and others. But I do know that I shall continue to write and say what I believe. I don't seek to be anyone's martyr or hero, but telling it like I think it is—that's the only way I know how to be me.

I Respect Cassius Clay Sincerely

During World War II, the US Army sought to court-martial Robinson on charges of insubordination related to an incident in which he refused to move to the back of a Jim Crow bus. Robinson was eventually acquitted of the charges and received an honorary discharge, fully confident that he had done the right thing in resisting the military's efforts to deny him first-class citizenship.

In spite of this personal history of principled dissent, Robinson, in the following column, takes a swipe at Muhammad Ali for having refused to follow draft laws. In June 1967, Ali was convicted of draft evasion, sentenced to five years in prison, and slapped with a ten-thousand-dollar fine. The boxer had claimed that his religion prohibited him from killing other men.

Robinson's son Jackie Jr. had served in Vietnam by this point, and Robinson believed that all young men should follow the example of his son and serve their country in a time of war. In the case of Ali, then, Robinson clearly sided with the government's case that Ali should abide by the draft laws in spite of his religion.

However much he claims to respect Ali in this column, Robinson certainly offers no support for the boxer's evasion of the draft. Nor does he respect the boxer enough to call him by the name he embraced shortly after converting to Islam in 1964.

      Source: New York Amsterdam News, October 14, 1967, 17.

DURING THE RAPID MARCH of recent events—the war developments, the explosions in our cities, the much-publicized activities of Rap Brown and Stokely Carmichael—people seem to have lost awareness of the heroism and tragedy of Muhammad Ali or Cassius Clay.

The conviction of Clay, following his refusal to submit to induction, came as no surprise to any of us, I am sure. I am convinced that before all the shouting is over, the five-year sentence will be reduced, although the charges will stick.

The plea by the prosecuting attorney that Clay's record has been a good one: that his problems began only a few years ago and that his contributions in winning the Olympic title and the heavyweight championship should be taken into consideration—all are significant. They imply that although the prosecution fought for conviction, they do not want Clay to go to jail. The threats that conviction would result in riots seem to have been empty threats.

In my view, the deposed champion has demonstrated that he is fighting for a principle. While I cannot agree with it, I respect him sincerely. He fully understood the penalty and price he would have to pay for taking his stand. He was willing and prepared to make the challenge out of his deeply rooted convictions. And he is ready to accept the consequences. This is his heroism—and I believe it to be genuine.

The tragedy is that an extremely talented young man has apparently allowed himself to be used. He had so very much to give, not only to the boxing profession, but to young, oppressed people this country over. He literally picked himself out of obscurity and made himself a champion. Then he tossed it away.

As I have said, I have no doubts about his sincerity. I do believe he has been badly advised and that he could have best served his cause by making his protest and then going on to obey the rules of the draft. He has a felony conviction now which will follow him all of his life.

He, in my view, has won a battle by standing up for his principle. But will he lose the war in terms of the greater contribution he could have made, based on his splendid career and prospects?

The United States Supreme Court overturned the conviction of Ali in an 8–0 vote in 1971.

LBJ Deserves Our Support on Vietnam

In April 1967, Robinson appeared on a television program and defended President Johnson's commitment to the Vietnam War (just as he does in this column). Robinson also mentioned his son Jackie's service in Vietnam and took issue with Black Power advocate Stokely Carmichael's advice to young African Americans considering their options in relation to the war. Here are several excerpts from the program:

> Stokely Carmichael certainly has a way of getting around the colleges and he talks to these young Negro kids about Vietnam and not going to war, and he has developed this slogan of "Hell no, I won't go." In my view the reason he says, "Hell no, I won't go," is that he is classified III-A or some such thing like that. He doesn't have to go. And he goes around and tells these youngsters not to go into the war, and I think this is wrong, because we can't select our activities. If we demand equal opportunity in this country, we have to accept the responsibility that goes with it, and one of those responsibilities, in my view, is participation in whatever our government is doing. . . .
>
> Well, if you're talking about Vietnam, I don't go along with the theory that we shouldn't be in Vietnam before we settle our problems. The president said the other day—and I would have to go by what he said—that we are spending more money on the poverty program in these United States than we are on the war in Vietnam. If this is true, he certainly hasn't pulled back in his determination to see that the problems are eliminated. What I like about the president is that even though his advisors were telling him not to involve himself in Civil Rights activities

at this point, he went back to Howard University, a Negro college in Washington, and said to the students there that the same thing I told you a year ago, my involvement in the civil rights movement, I am still involved in it. I still believe in it. I'm here to tell you I'm not pulling back at all. I believe that this is true. But I believe if we pull out of Vietnam, our commitments—commitments I believe that three Presidents have made—I think that we are in trouble. What I disagree with a lot of the people about in Vietnam is simply that they are blaming the United States for all of the atrocities. You hear stories about the violence of the Viet Cong, going in if they don't like what is going on, they bring women and children out and they kill them without any provocation. Certainly we have our problems. We have our faults, but we're not alone in it. I think that we've got to accuse the Viet Cong just as we accuse the United States. And I think our involvement is a moral commitment that we have to live up to. And I had a boy that was in there for one year and I didn't resent his going there. As a matter of fact, when he came back, he felt that he had made his contribution and he was pleased to have done it. I don't say that he is still pleased about it now because he returned to these United States and ran into the same kind of bigotry and prejudice that he had before he left. And it bothered him tremendously.[2]

Robinson was very proud of the military service that African Americans had contributed throughout US history and saw this service as evidence of commendable patriotism within the African American community and of concrete sacrifices that African Americans had made in order to strengthen democratic principles in the United States. Consider this excerpt from a column he had written in January 1963: "The American Negro today believes that America is his country. He believes he has a right to claim it as such. For he loves America and has consistently displayed his loyalty and patriotism to her. He has shown it under arms from the example of black Crispus Attucks, first patriot to die in the American Revolution, right down to Dorie

2. Transcript of interview with Theodore Granik, "Youth Wants to Know," April 1967, Jackie Robinson Papers, box 9, Library of Congress, Washington, DC.

Miller, the naval mess man who manned his ship's guns to shoot down Japanese aircraft in World War II."[3]

Source: New York Amsterdam News, October 21, 1967, 17.

I AM EXPERIENCING a growing concern about the increasing pressures being exerted in the attempt to persuade our president to halt the bombing in Vietnam. I have long admired Pennsylvania's Senator Hugh Scott for his courage. Senator Scott's recent statement unequivocally backing the president was in superb defiance of a mounting Republican "dove" trend.

"I am not a hawk," the senator declared. "But neither do I want to be a pigeon."

In my view, we shall certainly be in the pigeon position if Mr. Johnson places political expediency above his sacred trust and gives in to those who would halt the bombing. I wonder that so little is said of the reality that to stop the bombing would be to take a terrible gamble with the lives of our fighting men. They would be exposed to the possibility of becoming victims of an awful treachery of which the Viet Cong has already demonstrated itself capable.

I want to see our ground forces given the maximum of protection at all times. Although my wish for their safety extends to all of them whatever color, I must admit to an awareness that such a large percentage of the ground forces are Negroes.

It would be a tragedy indeed for us to find out the hard way that we had withdrawn vital protection from those ground forces only to suffer a recurrence of the double-cross the Viet Cong subjected us to earlier in this war. All of us recall the trusting forty-five day pause to which we agreed. During this respite, the Viet Cong made no effort to move toward peace. Instead, the enemy refortified itself and built more strength for the resumption of the fighting.

I have always believed the best defense is a good offense, especially in the kind of jungle fighting now going on. I am convinced that we must continue to deal from a position of strength. I have found this to be good

3. New York Amsterdam News, January 5, 1963, 9.

policy in athletics and I think it is probably the best policy in war. Should we cease to bomb the enemy's bridges, to destroy and cut off their ammunition bases, we would be extending them an open invitation to commit wholesale carnage of which our own fighting men would become the helpless victims.

President Johnson did not bring about this war. He is the third United States president whose policy has been one of helping the cause of South Vietnam. He is the third president who has acted out of conviction that it is far better to fight this fight in Vietnam than to wait until we must fight it closer to our shores.

I believe the president deserves the support and confidence of the American people on the Vietnam issue. Of us all, he is the one man bearing the most awesome burden when he seeks sleep at night or faces another day of heartbreaking responsibility. I believe that he yearns desperately for peace. But I believe that he is a man who will not be moved when he believes he is doing the best for his country. And I prayerfully hope he will not be moved.

Nevertheless, Robinson had mixed emotions about the war, especially when he, like so many others, began to see and feel the war's devastating effects on the nation's youth, including his own son. In a March 1968 letter to Nelson Rockefeller, Robinson wrote the following reflection on Johnson: "While, in my opinion, he has been the greatest influence in our domestic racial policies, he leaves so much to be desired on the foreign policy level."[4] Unfortunately, Robinson did not add any details to this significant criticism.

The Reconciling Faith of Martin Luther King Jr.

Riots erupted in several inner cities following the assassination of Martin Luther King Jr. on April 4, 1968. Fearing what they took to be the

---

4. Letter from Robinson to Nelson Rockefeller, March 27, 1968, Nelson A. Rockefeller Papers Personal, RG 4, series P, box 16, folder 393, Rockefeller Family Archives, Rockefeller Archive Center, Sleepy Hollow, New York.

worst—incessant riots, the emergence of Malcolm X as the main leader of African Americans, and increasing attacks on whites—frightened white politicians began to extol King and his calls for nonviolence and integration as they had never done before. But long before he died, Martin Luther King Jr. was Robinson's favorite civil rights leader of all time.

Source: New York Amsterdam News, April 13, 1968, 21.

BECAUSE I AM AN ETERNAL OPTIMIST, I have passed the first plateau of grief over the passing of the Rev. Dr. Martin Luther King, Jr.

I do not pretend that I have begun to reach the mountaintop which God showed the man who, in my view, was the greatest leader of the twentieth century.

But I have been able to come to regard his death as perhaps one of those great mysteries with which the Almighty moves—his wonders to perform.

I cannot claim to be a deeply religious man. So in order to reach this plateau, I have found it necessary to consult memory regarding the life of Dr. Martin King. I recall that in Montgomery, Alabama, Dr. King once preached a memorable sermon. The bus boycott that shook the conscience of the world was in progress.

After many months of sacrifice and miraculous unity of purpose on the part of 50,000 black citizens of Montgomery, it was believed that the bitter battle would be won. It would be only a matter of a little more time and allegiance to the nonviolent ethic.

Then one night a terrible event took place. Dr. King's home was bombed and even though his wife and baby daughter escaped injury, awful damage was done to the state of mind of the black community. For many of the citizens of Montgomery, nonviolence had become a way of life only because of their faith in their leader and their admiration for his commitment and dedication. Now, however, the life of that beloved leader had been jeopardized and the mood of black folk in Montgomery became ugly. By the thousands, they gathered in front of Dr. King's home that night.

There was agitation from some in the crowd to transform themselves into a mob. There were suggestions that they break up and arm themselves and meet again to visit retaliation upon the white community.

The mayor of Montgomery and the police chief appealed to the crowd to maintain calm. But the mood of the crowd grew uglier until Dr. King, who had rushed from his church to the scene in front of his home, suddenly appeared before them.

In that eloquent and commanding manner with which we are all so familiar, Dr. King pleaded with his people to go home and to desist from any rash or violent act until Sunday morning. He asked them to come to the Dexter Avenue Baptist Church Sunday and give him a chance to explain why nonviolence should continue.

That Sunday morning Dr. King preached a sermon: "God's Will and Man's Bombs." Where, he asked, was God in the midst of falling bombs? In sum, what he explained was that God has a dual nature. He is a God of two wills—a creative, redemptive, causal will, and a permissive will. When God made man, in order to give man true freedom, God had to allow man the power of choice between good and bad, Dr. King explained.

God is all-powerful and all good. . . . God never plans or creates evil, sickness or war or death or other sin. But sometimes God allows evil to exist in order to change the hearts and minds of men so that he can then exercise his creative, redemptive will.

So it was with the brothers who sought to slay Joseph. God did not plan murder. Joseph's brothers did that. But . . . after Joseph had been left for dead, God allowed him to escape to Egypt, to come to sit on the right hand of a powerful ruler and to be able to save from famine his father and the brothers who had sought to slay him.

Dr. King said that perhaps this was what God had done in Montgomery—allowed some bombs to fall, and some property to be destroyed, so that the white community could feel the necessity for reconciliation with the black community. History tells us that this is what happened in Montgomery.

Perhaps this will happen today in America. Perhaps, after the raging emotions quiet down. Perhaps, after the streets of our cities are no longer haunted by angry black people seeking revenge.

5

On Politics with Principles

Politics Is Sort of Like Baseball

Robinson stakes out an independent position in American politics—one that selects candidates simply on their record of "making democracy work." Nine months after writing the column excerpted here, Robinson heaped praise on his favorite Democratic candidate—Senator Hubert Humphrey. "From the very first, Humphrey has made it all too plain that his position is one of vigorous action and to assure every American of equal civil rights," Robinson wrote.[1]

Source: New York Post, May 8, 1959, 92.

BACK IN 1947 when I joined the Dodger baseball club, there were a couple of Dodgers who objected to Branch Rickey about my coming on the team. Later, however, they came to me to pass on tips as to how I might help win games.

Frankly, I don't think these particular players, within a short month or so, had changed their feelings toward me. It was just that they felt it would mean more money in their pockets if we could win.

Politics to me is somewhat similar to that situation—except that instead of money, it's votes.

The year 1960 is fast coming around, and all the politicians who have kept their distance since the last campaign are out in full force now—each with a big smile, a warm handshake and a hatful of promises. And I won't

1. *New York Post*, February 22, 1960, 36.

say that I never forgive, but like the proverbial old elephant, believe me, I don't forget!

I guess you'd call me an Independent, since I've never identified myself with one party or another in politics. As a Negro, I've been wooed by the Democrats with the memory of Franklin D. Roosevelt and the New Deal, and cultivated by the Republicans with the memory of Abraham Lincoln and the Civil War. But, like more and more people nowadays, I always decide my vote by taking as careful a look as I can at the actual candidates and issues themselves, no matter what the party label or the ancestral ghost.

And now that a presidential election is just around the corner, I'm giving careful scrutiny to the records of all the leading contenders to see what they've actually done, not so much what they say they'll do.

For instance, I would ask Gov. Rockefeller why he now insists he has to wait to see how New York City's law against discrimination in private housing comes along before he starts implementing his campaign promise to throw all his resources into enacting a similar measure on a state-wide level.

I'm remembering, too, the votes that Sen. Kennedy and some other Northern "liberals" cast to send the 1957 civil rights bill back to committee in a Southern-engineered attempt to kill any action by Congress to help Southern Negroes gain the equal voting rights promised them by the Constitution nearly ninety years ago. And I'm wondering just what was said by and to this same senator behind closed doors at the Southern Governors Conference that resulted in his emerging as the fair-haired boy of the Dixie politicians.

And I think I'd want a fuller report about the reasons the President's Committee on Government Contracts, headed by Vice President Nixon, has largely been so ineffectual in enforcing provisions in federal contracts that are supposed to bar racial discrimination in hiring and in upgrading in any company doing work for the government.

Since I believe Adlai Stevenson has as good a chance as any, I'd have to mull over his marked soft-pedaling of civil rights issues when he was actively seeking delegates' votes to insure his re-nomination in Chicago in 1956.

I certainly don't want to give the impression that during the elections Negro voters will be considering only what's best for Negroes alone. As Americans, we have as much stake in this country as anyone else. We, too, are concerned about foreign policy, farm policy, national defense, a balanced budget, and all the rest.

Still, to effectively participate in a democracy, you must first enjoy the basic freedoms that democracy guarantees to everyone else. And since Negroes, North and South, have so long been deprived of many of the rights that everyone else takes for granted, it's only natural that we are especially interested in catching up on basic freedoms before we work up much excitement about protective tariffs or forest preserves or the like.

Then, too, Negroes aren't seeking anything which is not good for the nation as well as ourselves. In order for America to be 100 percent strong— economically, defensively and morally—we cannot afford the waste of having second and third class citizens.

Negro citizens this year and next will be using their individual, unpledged votes as never before. No one party or candidate can lay safe prior claim to the so-called "Negro vote." It is for the parties and candidates to demonstrate themselves that they are actually helping to make democracy work—not just for white people, nor just for colored people, but for each one of us separately and for all of us collectively.

Certainly this is no more than any voter has a right to expect, and a duty to demand.

When a Man Has His Foot on Your Throat, Changing His Heart Can Come Later

At this point in his life, there was nothing in politics that disappointed Robinson more than President Eisenhower's calls for "patience" when dealing with the issue of civil rights.[2] Just a year before he wrote the following article,

---

2. See, for instance, W. H. Lawrence, "President Urges Patience in Crisis," *New York Times* (NYT), September 11, 1957, 25.

Robinson had attended the Summit Meeting of Negro Leaders in Washing-
ton, DC, and followed up with a note to the president. "I was sitting in the
audience at the Summit Meeting of Negro Leaders yesterday when you said
we must have patience," Robinson penned. "On hearing you say this, I felt
like standing up and saying, 'Oh no! Not again.' I respectfully remind you,
sir, that we have been the most patient of all people."³

Robinson refers below to an all-white jury's decision in Monroe, North
Carolina, to acquit a white man charged with attempting to rape an African
American woman. After the jury had returned its verdict, Robert Williams,
the head of the Union County, North Carolina, NAACP, expressed his frus-
tration by saying that, since African Americans could not get justice in the
courts, they should "meet violence with violence" and even "be willing to kill
if necessary."⁴

Source: New York Post, June 12, 1959, 92.

PRESIDENT EISENHOWER, speaking before a conference called by the
Civil Rights Commission in Washington this week, said he based his hopes
in the civil rights area on "moral law rather than statutory law, because I
happen to be one of those people who has very little faith in the ability of
statutory law to change the human heart, or to eliminate prejudice.

Well, I'm certainly in agreement with Mr. Eisenhower that laws alone
will not change people's personal feelings. But it is also evident that something more than patience is called for when we haven't made much progress with moral law in some sections of the country.

When, for instance, a white man can brutally beat and criminally
assault a Negro woman in full view of her children and other witnesses,
and arrogantly boast, "Go ahead and call the law—they won't do anything
to me!" and be set scot-free by the all-white jury—such as happened in
Monroe, N.C., a few weeks ago—then it is obvious that moral as well as
statutory law is being brazenly flouted and ignored.

3. Letter from Robinson to Dwight Eisenhower, May 13, 1958, Dwight D. Eisenhower
Papers, Official File, box 731, folder 142-A, Dwight D. Eisenhower Library, Abilene, Kansas.
   4. "NAACP Leader Urges Violence," NYT, May 7, 1959, 22.

Can the president possibly mean that we must go ahead and allow these people to commit these crimes and merely stand and wait, and hope and pray, that their hearts will change?

The president should be told that Negroes aren't nearly as worried at this stage of the game about eliminating prejudice as they are about eliminating the kind of overt, vicious acts of violence which our newspapers have been filled with lately. When a man has his foot on your throat, you can worry later on about changing his heart. Right now, your main concern is to keep him from choking you, else you may never live to save his soul.

When the president of the United States repeatedly says that people's hearts must be changed to insure equal opportunity, he effectively encourages bigots to take free license in their campaign of terror and intimidation. I'm reminded of the old story about locking the barn door after the horse has been stolen. When people's hearts have changed, we won't need a law. But until they do, we must have means of keeping people from violating the rights of others. And I submit that the president's reliance on moral law has failed to do the job.

If the president is worried about the effects of civil rights legislation on the "good" people of the South, then his fears are needless. Any decent citizen, North or South, need not fear the penalties of a just law, so long as he doesn't violate it. And make no mistake about it: the vast majority of the people of the South have proven they are law abiding and will live within the law and the court decisions if given encouragement and protected from the actively vicious element. I think the recent hopeful signs in Little Rock and other places are proof of that.

As I pointed out earlier this week, it often takes a long time for people to weed out their deeply ingrained prejudices. If the president would merely review the record, he would discover that Negroes have been patient for nigh on to 96 years, since Abraham Lincoln signed the Emancipation Proclamation. But now we are tired of waiting for others' hearts to change before receiving our rights. We are convinced that this patience must now be firmly backed up with enforcement of existing laws, and enactment of new ones where necessary.

It was quite evident to me, when I saw the TV newsreels of the president delivering his speech, that he was talking "off the cuff." These, then, are undoubtedly his own personal feelings on the matter. But it seems to me that Mr. Eisenhower must realize he is the president of all the people, regardless of what his personal feelings are. It is his sworn duty, as chief executive, to see to it that laws are enacted and enforced to protect the welfare of those who cannot protect themselves, whether other people's hearts have changed or not. Since when has our democracy fallen to so low an ebb that the president must hesitate in his duties because he doubts that Americans will obey the law?

In a letter to me last year, Dwight D. Eisenhower made the following statement:

"I am firmly on record as believing that every citizen—of every race and creed—deserves to enjoy equal civil rights and liberties, for there can be no such citizen in a democracy as a half-free citizen."

How long, Mr. President, must we continue to wait before you back up those fine and singing words with definite, positive action?

I Admired Castro's Passion, but He's Misidentified the Enemy

In 1959 Fidel Castro led a guerrilla insurgency that toppled the corrupt government of Cuban president Fulgencio Batista. After the revolution, Castro sought to undermine US domination of the Cuban economy and to establish diplomatic relations with the Soviet Union. On January 1, 1960, however, Castro also took part in a banquet to which the Cuban Institute of Tourism had invited a group of US celebrities, including Joe Louis, as part of an effort to revitalize the island's collapsing tourism industry.

Source: New York Post, January 13, 1960, 92.

FIDEL CASTRO held a dinner in Havana recently to which he invited a number of American celebrities. The apparent purpose of this affair was to inject some life into Cuba's declining tourist trade. Though one wire service reported that I was in attendance at Castro's banquet-table, the fact is that I not only did not attend but I was not even invited.

Somewhat peeved by this report, I wrote to Prime Minister Castro last week. Though I doubt Castro himself had any hand in this, I felt it was but another instance of an alarming state of irresponsibility which has come to characterize the Castro regime since the Cuban revolution a year ago. And so I wrote that I hoped the Prime Minister would not mind if I addressed a word or two to him concerning one man's opinion of the currently sad state of Cuban-American relations.

I am aware, of course, of the difficult position that any of the smaller nations here in the Americas find themselves in, when confronted by the size, wealth and power of the United States. I am aware, also, that regardless of size, each sovereign nation has the right and duty to determine the course of its own affairs, without interference from the U.S. or any other nation. Still, as I told Castro, I can't help but feel that his present course of seemingly deliberate antagonism towards this country amounts to cutting off his nose to spite his face.

Since U.S. tourism has long been one of Cuba's chief industries, it stands to reason that Castro cannot expect to attack the U.S. day after day and still expect our tourists to flock to Cuba on vacations. The casinos, I am told, are nearly empty. And though Castro has tried to entice visitors by promising to pay half their fares to Cuba from Miami, Cuba's hotels are far from crowded, and the plush restaurants and nightclubs are not attracting the Yankee dollars Cuba needs to keep its economy sound.

In my letter to Castro, I pointed out how favorable an impression he had made when he visited the U.S. shortly after his successful revolution. Undoubtedly, Cuba needed a change of government, and many of us here admired Castro for his passion and zeal in fighting against the previous regime. That this impression has had a severe setback since is greatly unfortunate, for it is Cuba that is suffering as a result of it.

I told Castro I felt his hopes and aspirations for the Cuban people would be better served if he could find some other way of dealing with our government than his present course. Self-righteous as he may feel his position to be, he will accomplish little by going at it as if he were still fighting in a revolution. As much as we have admired his spirit, no one is going to offer him the aid he seeks if he continues to treat us as if we were his worst enemies.

I have visited Cuba, and I know the Cubans to be fine and friendly people. They deserve a better break than they've gotten in past years. They supported Castro's revolt in search of that better break. But now, there are growing threats of revolt against Castro unless a more realistic approach to their problem is found.

It's nice to have a press party and announce that a lot of U.S. celebrities were there, but there comes a time when facts must be faced, and squarely. I suggest, for the sake of the Cuban people, that Fidel Castro stop now to see where he is going rather than continue to plunge along blindly. Passion and zeal are fine qualities. But a dose of foresight is a pretty good commodity to have along with them.

Next Chief Executive Must Be More than Amateur Golfer

On May 1, 1960, a US spy plane piloted by Francis Gary Powers was shot down over the Soviet Union. The US government initially responded to the incident by claiming that a weather plane had gotten lost and crashed somewhere in the Soviet Union. But Soviet premier Nikita Khrushchev happily embarrassed the United States by presenting a bit of counterevidence: wreckage from the spy plane, Powers himself, and some of the results of his espionage. Much to his chagrin, President Eisenhower backtracked and conceded to his main opponent in the Cold War.

Robinson uses the U-2 plane incident as yet another opportunity to criticize President Eisenhower. Doing so, Jackie delivers one of his best lines ever about golf.

Source: New York Post, May 18, 1960, 96.

THE FIASCO of the Paris summit conference should and must be the concern of every one of us here in the U.S. and throughout the world. For the explosive breakdown in relations between the world's two major powers over the incredible spy-plane incident has placed us all closer to another world war than anything since Korea. And, as everybody knows, the next such conflagration may well be the last—ever.

The fact that Khrushchev is exploiting to the hilt the situation that the U.S. administration's blundering has placed us in has brought calls from many quarters for "solidarity" behind President Eisenhower. Certainly, none of us wishes to make any more difficult the extremely delicate task of bringing things back to even the unsatisfactory cold-war level we've been living on for years. But I think it is the right and duty of each of us to look long and hard at the situation we're in, and to call a spade a spade.

For we can no longer worry about saving face. We must worry about saving humanity.

The overriding fact is this: no matter how much our national leaders and our press try to protect the administration regarding the U-2 plane incident, it was a damaging blow to our national prestige and honor that may take years to overcome.

Certainly, whoever was responsible for taking the chance of such a flight over Russia knew they were playing with fire. But the report that President Eisenhower himself didn't know about the flight until afterwards is the most damaging news of all. For this points up all the more why President Eisenhower should stay away from his Jim Crow golf club in Augusta, Ga., and devote more time to doing the job he was elected to do. No matter how many excuses are made for him, as chief executive he must bear full responsibility. And to be caught in the embarrassing position that he has is damaging not only to him personally, but to all America and the free world.

Khrushchev's bullying tactics in forcing an end to the summit conference are justly resented and deplored by all of us. His facetious statement that, "As God is my witness, my hands are clean and my soul is pure," will not fool anyone. It is no secret that the Soviet spy apparatus is working as hard as our own to obtain all the information it can, by whatever means it can.

But this cannot be made an excuse for a diplomatic blunder of the first order by our own administration. No ringing calls for "solidarity" should blind any of us to the basic fact of the matter. Our next chief executive must be more than an amateur golfer. He must also be President.

Nixon May Not Go Slow

After Humphrey dropped out of the 1960 presidential race, Robinson switched horses, landing on none other than Republican candidate Richard

Nixon. Robinson was attracted to Nixon because of the vice president's viru-
lent opposition to communism, his public statement that the fight against
communism abroad was directly related to the quest for civil rights at home,
his willingness to tour Africa, his leadership in passing the 1957 civil rights
legislation, and his apparent sense that President Eisenhower was moving
too slowly on civil rights. Given his distaste for John F. Kennedy, whom he
considered to be pragmatic rather than principled, Robinson would later
find it rather easy to leave behind his job as a columnist for the "New York
Post" and take up full-time work in Nixon's campaign.
Source: New York Post, May 23, 1960, 72.

EARLY THIS MONTH I went down to Washington for a luncheon meeting with Vice President Nixon, Attorney General Rogers and Labor Secretary Mitchell. Several times during the past few years the Vice President
and I have had occasion to exchange correspondence. This meeting developed out of my wish to talk with him personally about my concern—and
that of many of my acquaintances—for the importance of civil rights in
the coming presidential elections.

From the frank and open discussion we had in Washington, I came
away with a number of impressions. First, Nixon seems very much aware
of the need for using the influence and prestige of the presidency to
advance equal rights and human dignity. He is aware also that great effort
will be needed to overcome the conservatives in his own party who have
continually aligned themselves with Southern Democrats to stymie civil
rights progress. Nixon left me with the sincere feeling that if he becomes
president, he will use the influence of the office and overcome these
obstacles.

Secondly, I felt that in allying himself with men such as Rogers and
Mitchell, Nixon has the advantage of having able, enlightened associates
and advisors. Both are men with whom I was greatly impressed, and I
couldn't help suspecting that they have long been chafing under the conservative, go-slow policies of the present occupant of the White House.

Nixon, I think, is in a similar position himself. As vice president, he has
been rather in the position of executive assistant. I predict that if he moves
into the top spot, he will then prove he has the ability and that he has grown

tremendously during the past seven years. Add that to his interest in civil rights and I feel he has as good a chance as any of the current candidates to woo and win a great many Negro votes—*if not a better chance.*

While words are important, actions, of course, are what count in the final analysis. And many of us will be watching the vice president with even closer scrutiny in the months to come, both before the expected nomination and afterwards. There are still questions in my mind concerning Nixon, as there are concerning every other current candidate. I feel, for instance, that he can no longer wait to begin making his own position unmistakably clear—on civil rights and other issues—and to disengage himself from the restraint of supporting Eisenhower policies with which he may not be in full accord. For, while he has convinced me and others of his sincerity, there are a great many skeptics waiting to be shown.

Since Sen. Humphrey has dropped from the race, on the basis of my observations so far I feel Richard Nixon has many of the qualities I have been looking for in a presidential candidate. And I can see no reason why I, for one, should not give very careful consideration to supporting him for the presidency.

Kennedy Ruthless Against Negroes in Quest for Power

Robinson, unlike many African American voters in the 1960 presidential election, did not find himself warming up to John F. Kennedy. Robinson was troubled by several matters about the senator from Massachusetts—his vote to send the 1957 civil rights bill back to committee in a southern-engineered attempt to kill the legislation, his private breakfast with segregationist governor John Patterson of Alabama (who called Kennedy "a friend of the South" right after the meeting),[5] and his failure to be an outspoken advocate of and participant in the civil rights movement. On a related point, Robinson was not a fan of Lyndon Johnson at this point, either. Johnson would never admit

5. "Alabama Governor Endorses Kennedy," NYT, June 17, 1959, 38.

Robinson into his close circle of friends, even after Jackie campaigned for him in 1964, and perhaps some of his reasons lie in Robinson's 1960 columns.

The Kennedy campaign team sought a truce with Robinson, and mutual friend Chet Bowles, the former governor of Connecticut, arranged for Jackie to meet with Kennedy at Bowles's home in Georgetown. The meeting did not go well, though, and Robinson left feeling that he could not trust Kennedy, primarily because, according to Robinson, JFK refused to look him in the eye and conceded that he was basically unfamiliar with African Americans and their concerns.

In the following column, Robinson refers to Thurgood Marshall, director-counsel of the NAACP Legal Defense and Educational Fund, Inc., and future Supreme Court justice, and Samuel Englehardt, a state senator from Alabama and chair of Alabama's Democratic Executive Committee. Englehardt had accompanied his fellow segregationist Governor John Patterson to the infamous breakfast with John Kennedy.

Source: New York Post, July 15, 1960, 60.

THE GREAT STRIDES the Democrats made with the adoption of the strongest civil rights plank in history have, in my opinion, been recklessly jeopardized by the addition of Lyndon Johnson to the ticket as vice-presidential nominee.

Though everybody knows politics makes strange bedfellows, if Sen. Kennedy thinks liberals, minorities, and Negro voters in particular, will take to the idea of lying down with him and Johnson—even on so strong a plank—I think he is due for a rude awakening. Obviously Kennedy hopes to offset the plank in the eyes of Southern segregationists by choosing Johnson as a running mate, but even this seems likely to backfire. Thus Kennedy's both-sides-of-the-fence politicking has got him in trouble with both sides now, and he has lost ground on each.

When I flew to Washington two weeks ago to meet with Sen. Kennedy at his request, I pointed out to him that he should not count on offsetting a wrong with a right insofar as Negro voters are concerned. A luncheon with Thurgood Marshall has by no means erased the image of his fateful breakfast with Alabama's Gov. Patterson and White Citizens Council head

Sam Englehardt. Nor, I predict, will a high-sounding platform counterbal-ance—in the eyes of those who constitute the balance of power in many of the key Northern states—this obvious bid to please the Democrats.

I've listened to the reasons given to support this action. Johnson's removal from the leadership of the Senate will help to speed civil rights action, I've been told. The vice-presidency is largely a ceremonial office and, in effect, Johnson has been "kicked upstairs." Granted, these may be beneficial byproducts. But basically and principally, Johnson's nomination is a bid for the appeasement of Southern bigots—just as the Patterson break-fast, the vote with the Southerners to send the 1957 civil rights bill to die in Eastland's committee, and a long list of other Kennedy actions have been.

What this sell-out reveals about Kennedy is a naked, damaging truth: Kennedy is willing to ruthlessly gamble with the rights—and the very lives—of millions of Southern Negro Americans in order to satisfy his own personal ambition to be President. . . .

If faced with the choice of a Democratic ticket whose presidential nominee has been playing both sides of the fence—and whose vice-presidential nominee is a proven segregationist—and a Republican ticket whose head has a better-than-average civil rights record—and whose sec-ond man will not likely be a Dixiecrat—I know how I, for one, shall cast my vote in November.

I do not pretend to speak for anyone else. But I have a hunch I'm going to have plenty of company.

Statesman John F. Kennedy Reelected

After Kennedy was elected president, Robinson remained a steadfast critic, faulting the president for not being assertive enough in the field of civil rights. On May 7, 1963, for example, Robinson sent a telegram to President Kennedy in response to police commissioner Eugene "Bull" Connor's ill-fated decision to sic dogs and turn high-pressured fire hoses on schoolchildren who had joined the demonstrations in Birmingham, Alabama. "I submit," Robinson wired, "that you do have the power to cut off federal expenditures within a state which has become a police state and to declare martial law for the purpose of guaranteeing the safety of American citizens."⁶ Robinson was pleased when President Kennedy eventually ordered federal troops to Birmingham, and he seemed even more delighted when the president delivered his famous civil rights speech on June 11. With its remarkably positive tone, the column reveals a side that the public did not often see of the political Jackie Robinson—a side that warmly embraced politicians who would fight for first-class citizenship for all Americans, even those politicians with whom he had fiercely battled.

Source: New York Amsterdam News, June 22, 1963, 11.

AS AN AMERICAN CITIZEN, I am deeply proud of our president. In my opinion, the address which Mr. Kennedy made to the American people on the color question is one of the finest declarations ever issued in the cause of human rights.

As consistent readers of this column know, I have been highly critical of this administration and its handling of the civil rights issue.

I must state now that I believe the president has come through with statesmanship, with courage, with wisdom and absolute sincerity.

Speaking as one person, I can honestly say that Mr. Kennedy has now done everything I hoped he would do.

I expressed that sentiment in a telegram which I sent to the White House—a telegram in which I said to Mr. Kennedy:

"Thank you for emerging as the most forthright president we have ever had and for providing us with the inspired leadership that we so desperately needed. I am more proud than ever of my American heritage."

This column believes that Mr. Kennedy's message to the nation is a document which every American ought to study thoughtfully.

I liked the way he called upon each of us to "examine his conscience." I liked the way he pointed out that racial injustice is contrary to the principles upon which America was founded and observed that "the rights of every man are diminished when the rights of one man are threatened."

6. Letter from Robinson to John Kennedy, May 7, 1963, Jackie Robinson Papers, box 5, folder 14, Library of Congress, Washington, DC.

The president, in this message, did eloquently what many of us felt he ought to do for some time. He addressed himself to the "moral issues involved in the denial of rights to every human."

The moral issue involved, Mr. Kennedy stated, "is as old as the Scriptures and as clear as the American Constitution."

He expressed his concern for the kind of image we present on the international scene. He added how much more important it is to stop and realize what we are saying to each other through our conduct and treatment of fellow humans.

"Are we saying," the president asked, "that this is the land of the free except for the Negroes; that we have no second-class citizens except Negroes; that we have no class system or caste system, no ghettos, no master race, except with respect to Negroes?

"Now the time has come," Mr. Kennedy continued, "for the nation to fulfill its promise."

Well, President Kennedy has fulfilled his promise. He was not only speaking, however. He had acted that same day, throwing the weight of the government behind the two Negro students who Governor Wallace attempted to ban from Alabama State University. He pledged even more significant action through proposal of sweeping civil rights reforms to Congress.

Mr. Kennedy's address was not the speech of a politician. It was the pronouncement of a statesman. Yet, I agree with my wife, who said to me: "Tonight, Mr. Kennedy was re-elected."

Our Fallen President

Although he had been a tough critic at times, Robinson had grown to admire President Kennedy for his emerging commitment to civil rights, especially after JFK delivered his historic June 11, 1963, speech in response to brutal police tactics against black children in Birmingham, Alabama. In this column, written shortly after Kennedy's assassination, Robinson even describes the president as "a noble man."

Robinson also refers below to Medgar Evers, the civil rights activist who was murdered outside his home in Jackson, Mississippi, just after attending a civil rights meeting and just after Kennedy had delivered his June 11 speech. As the NAACP field secretary in Mississippi, Evers had engineered the courageous campaign to eliminate segregation in Jackson. Committed to a nonviolent campaign, Evers used sit-ins, demonstrations, boycotts, and mass meetings—methods that white segregationists nevertheless found overly antagonistic and threatening.

Source: New York Amsterdam News, *December 7, 1963, 13.*

WHEN THE TRAGIC NEWS FIRST HIT, like millions of Americans, I gasped with disbelief that here in America in 1963, a president could be murdered simply because he was a man of courageous conviction. What a tragic year this has been, with two great Americans—John Kennedy and Medgar Evers—paying the supreme sacrifice because they had given the last full measure of devotion.

A noble man is gone. This was a man whom I often criticized. But I was thrilled to write in this column several months ago that, in my opinion, the president had emerged as the chief executive who has done more for the civil rights cause than any other president. I had been critical of him because I believed that strong pressure must be applied by those of us who believe in human dignity since such strong pressure was being exerted by those who do not. In these last few months, I have felt a deep admiration for the courage of Mr. Kennedy, so much so that one of his top aides said to me recently: "Jack, you are certainly in his corner now, aren't you?"

My deep concern for the maintenance of a two-party system would have led me to campaign for Nelson Rockefeller had he received the GOP nomination. But, truthfully, I had the feeling that the president would have been reelected. If this happened, I would have had no fears about the progress of the civil rights struggle under his administration.

If the Democratic Party chooses President Lyndon Johnson as its standard-bearer in 1964, and if the Republicans select Barry Goldwater, where will the Negro stand? I wish our new president every good wish in the tough job he faces. But I am not convinced, despite his fine work with equal job opportunity or his wonderful speeches about equality, that Lyndon Johnson could sufficiently shrug off the old Southern traditions and pressures to the extent that our fight for freedom will move ahead. I think I know where Barry Goldwater stands.

That is why I believe it is imperative that the Republican Party line up behind the banner of Nelson Rockefeller. If the GOP does this, the Democrats will have to seek to find someone who will surely carry on the struggle for human rights with the devotion and bravery which characterized our fallen president. I hope that serious and somber thought will be given to this.

The GOP: Too White?

Robinson was frustrated by what he took to be a systematic effort among Republicans to dismiss the possibility of winning a significant portion of African American voters. He sensed this dismissal not only when he campaigned for Richard Nixon but especially in 1961, when Senator Goldwater made the following claim: "We're not going to get the Negro vote as a bloc in 1964 and 1968, so we ought to go hunting where the ducks are."[7] Robinson believed that this type of sentiment betrayed the Republican legacy of Abraham Lincoln, undermined his own hope for a two-party system that would see both parties actively courting African American voters, and made it impossible for him to find a place in a party whose policies and practices he otherwise admired. Robinson would eventually become a Republican in the (relatively) liberal tradition of Nelson Rockefeller and George Romney. Robinson had used his May 4 column to write an "open letter" that warned Nixon of the dangers of dismissing the African American vote—and revealed the beginnings of Robinson's split from his former candidate of choice. The following is an excerpt of that letter.
Source: New York Amsterdam News, May 4, 1963, 11.

---

7. See the introduction, n. 5.

I HAVE TO SAY SORROWFULLY, however, that there is a strong question in my mind as to whether I would again support you or a candidate with your blessing.

I say this because I am deeply disturbed about a United Press International dispatch which quotes you as saying that you believe civil rights will not be the prime 1964 political issue in the South. I know that you have said you will not be a candidate but that you intend to exert some influence over party policy, platform and choice of candidate.

If quoted correctly, you are counseling the 1964 front-runner to take it easy on civil rights and to attempt to carry the South on a platform of economic conservatism. If quoted correctly, you reveal that you have learned nothing from your experience in the last Presidential campaign.

Evidently you are not persuaded, as many others are, that no man will become President of the United States in this day and time, who does not have the confidence of the Negro voter and the millions of decent Americans who believe in our democracy.

I Would Love to Be a Republican, but Barry Goldwater Is a Bigot

A few weeks after this column appeared in print, Goldwater sent Robinson a letter requesting a private meeting during which he could explain his stance on civil rights. Robinson declined the meeting in a written reply that excoriated the senator's appeal to states' rights when opposing federal civil rights legislation. Robinson also released both letters to the media.

Source: New York Amsterdam News, July 4, 1964, 19.

. . . I WILL SAY THAT, personally, I never could nor never will buy Barry Goldwater. In my opinion, he is a bigot, an advocate of white supremacy and more dangerous than Governor Wallace. If Senator Goldwater announced a change in views, I would not believe in him. I would believe that he was trying to calm down some of the terrific opposition which his racist statements and attitudes have brought down upon him from members of his own party.

When I think of Senator Goldwater and the statements he has made and the positions he has taken in voting as a member of Congress, I cannot help but relate these words and votes to the terrible nightmares which are taking place in Mississippi and St. Augustine, Florida.

When I think of Barry Goldwater, I cannot help remembering that the Justice Department has publicly expressed its concern as to how well a civil rights bill can work when the leading candidate for nomination of a major political party has expressed his opposition to it. The senator says he doesn't believe in the bill, but that if he were president, he would administer it. How naïve does he think the American people are?

I would love to be a Republican.

It isn't because I love the Republican Party.

It is because I feel that the only way we will get our freedom as Negroes—and thereby redeem the soul of America and make her fit to lead the free world—is if we have a two-party system. If we do not have a two-party system, there will be no competition for our vote. And a vote is as important to a politician as a dollar is to a baseball player who discovers that he doesn't mind playing ball with a Negro who can help win the pennant.

Barry Goldwater has shown contempt for the Negro people. In so doing, he has shown contempt for the principle with which the Republican Party is supposedly allied.

I can't tell you what to do. But I wish I could persuade you to do as I intend to do. If the Republican Party nominates Goldwater, I intend to work hard for the election of Lyndon B. Johnson. . . .

I would do it because, whether Mr. Goldwater knows it or not, this is my country too. What good is a civil rights bill in a country presided over by a man who doesn't want to agree with the convictions which Abraham Lincoln thought were right? . . .

I am a Negro first because, down through the centuries, we have proven that we are the most loyal Americans.

If I stood idly by and did nothing to help defeat Mr. Goldwater and what he stands for, I would not only become a traitor to myself and to my children but also to my race and to my country.

Give Johnson a Chance

Robinson publicized his change of heart about Lyndon Johnson, who had begun to speak out forcefully on behalf of civil rights and had negotiated successful passage of the Civil Rights Act of 1964. In a letter he sent to Hubert Humphrey ten days before this column was published, Robinson wrote that "if Mr. Johnson is sincere on civil rights, it will be a wonderful thing because there is no better friend to this cause than a converted Southerner."[8]
Source: New York Amsterdam News, August 29, 1964, 19.

. . . SOME OF THE LETTERS I have received have caused me grave concern. These are from people who say that they cannot vote for Goldwater but who also feel that they cannot support Johnson. They assert that Mr. Johnson's civil rights record, up until 1960, was much less than to be desired. What will these people do, then? I fear that they will stay away from the polls, not realizing that, by doing so, they will be helping Goldwater.

To them I would say that I cannot—nor would I—whitewash the fact that the LBJ civil rights record prior to 1960 was a bad one. But isn't it better to have a man who, in 1964, is both saying and doing bold and forthright things in civil rights than to entrust our future to a man who claims he had a good civil rights record in the past but who, in 1964, seeks to gain the presidency by capitalizing on white resentment to Negro demands for justice.

Furthermore, as I have often stated, I am opposed to Barry Goldwater not only because I consider him an enemy of our cause as Negroes, but also because I am frankly afraid to see the country led by such a man. Without national security and the preservation of world peace, civil rights for the Negro is a meaningless phrase.

I beg and implore every Negro citizen who is against Goldwater not to aid and abet his campaign by staying home from the polls. President

8. Robinson to Hubert Humphrey, August 14, 1964, Hubert H. Humphrey Papers, Senatorial Files, Control Files, 1964, 150.A.13.1 (B), Minnesota Historical Society, St. Paul, Minnesota.

Johnson has demonstrated some firm and sane leadership since he inherited the mantle of the presidency. Let's give him a chance, as the elected choice of the nation, to continue. For God's sake, and for America's, let's not put the reins of government into the hands of a man who doesn't seem to know, from day to day, exactly what he believes.

Let's register and vote—and get as many friends and relatives and neighbors to do the same. Let's back Johnson and buck Barry.

Seeing Through the Kennedy Glamour

Robinson had occasionally applauded Robert Kennedy for having spoken and acted on behalf of civil rights during his brother's administration, but he was intensely displeased with Kennedy's decision to move to New York in an effort to unseat the incumbent US senator, Kenneth Keating, a friend of Robinson and a racially progressive Republican.

Source: New York Amsterdam News, September 19, 1964, 15.

. . . IT IS INCONCEIVABLE to this writer that New Yorkers will be so blinded by the Kennedy glamour that they will forget the splendid job which has been done over the years by Senator Keating.

Most fair-minded people will concede that the former attorney general did an overall outstanding job while his brother was reigning in the White House. Yet it cannot be truthfully said that his record is spotless or perfectly consistent in defense of the rights of Negro people.

Let us not forget the several occasions when the civil rights struggle was at its height in crucial areas and Robert Kennedy seriously undercut the position of the civil rights leadership by calling for the Negro to "go slow."

Let us not forget that, as chief officer of the Justice Department, Bob Kennedy was the boss of J. Edgar Hoover, the head of the F.B.I. Mr. Kennedy has been credited with standing up to Mr. Hoover on several issues, but not (to our memory) on the issue of the F.B.I.'s miserable failure in the protection of Negro victims of Southern brutality and killings. The almost unbroken F.B.I. record of coming up with blanks in solving civil rights murders and church bombings did not measurably improve under Bob Kennedy.

Let us not forget either that there were several instances when monstrous crimes were committed against the Negro, and that when appealed to by the Negro leadership, Mr. Kennedy contended, as he did when the three youngsters were murdered in Mississippi, that the Justice Department had no jurisdiction. Some fine legal minds have countered this claim that the government has no authority to protect the constitutional rights of its citizens and to safeguard their liberty and their lives.

Recently when we returned from a trip to St. Augustine, Florida, where we had learned directly from the lips of Dr. King and his aides how little protection the government was giving to them against roving, segregationist murder gangs, we warned the attorney general, a plea which has gone unanswered to this day.

He has been awfully silent on such vital matters since the death of his brother and we have been at a loss to know why. . . .

Kennedy, much to Robinson's dismay, soundly defeated Keating.

RFK
A Knight in Shining Armor—for Mississippi

Robinson refers to a mind-boggling decision by Esther Carter, a US commissioner in Meridian, Mississippi, to dismiss charges against suspects in the murders of civil rights workers Michael Schwerner, James Chaney, and Andrew Goodman. She delivered this shocking decision after she had already refused to accept a signed confession obtained by the FBI. After Carter dismissed the charges, the Department of Justice found itself having to ask W. Harold Cox, a federal district judge and a segregationist, to reconvene a grand jury to hear charges against the suspects.
Source: New York Amsterdam News, December 26, 1964, 9.

AS WAS TO BE EXPECTED—and, in fact, was predicted by our top civil rights leaders—the sovereign state of Mississippi has once more found a way to thwart justice, despite FBI arrests in connection with the Goodman-Chaney-Schwerner murders.

You can count on Mississippi to demonstrate its consistent defiance of our national government.

One wonders how we will ever be able to enforce the new civil rights act when so often the fate of the accused is left in the hands of friends and neighbors who would rather uphold the doctrine of white supremacy than to discharge the demands of justice. In this case, a Mississippi woman commissioner, not even an attorney, handed down what the Justice Department has termed an unprecedented ruling, in order to free the apprehended parties.

Now the Justice Department is in the position of having to ask Judge Cox, an avowed segregationist, to summon those freed before a grand jury. As it appears, the jurors would be segregationists. The jury would be all-white. The judge would be a segregationist. . . .

It is ironic that the Justice Department must now turn to a man like Judge Cox. As former attorney general—and head of that department—the now Senator-elect Robert Kennedy once went on record stalwartly defending his late brother's appointments of segregationists to the federal bench. Mr. Kennedy was quite vocal in that defense. Yet we have not heard from him with regard to the latest Mississippi travesty on justice which involves families of his new constituency. Neither, by the way, did we hear from the former attorney general when Mr. Hoover accused Dr. Martin King of being a "notorious liar."

Robert Kennedy is not unlike other members of the breed of politicians. As long as the electorate is gullible, politicians get away with anything they can. So long as the Negro citizen continues to allow himself to be fooled in the belief that Mr. Kennedy is really a pure knight in shining armor tilting against injustice, then Mr. Kennedy will continue to be silent when he should speak. . . .

Nelson Rockefeller
Not One of the Far-Out, Right-Wing Kooks, Goons, and Bigots

Nelson Rockefeller—a moderate, racially progressive, probusiness, and anti-Goldwater Republican—was Robinson's favorite politician in 1966. Fewer things in politics pleased Robinson more than the time Rockefeller stood firm as Goldwater delegates booed and jeered him during his convention speech at the 1964 Republican National Convention.

Source: New York Amsterdam News, January 8, 1966, 11.

A NUMBER OF PEOPLE of my acquaintance, more of them Democrats than Republicans, agree with me that one of the finest hours in the life of Governor Nelson Rockefeller occurred at the Republican National Convention in San Francisco in 1964.

It was indeed a classic and splendid sight to observe this man standing tall in a hostile atmosphere, fighting with all the vigor and eloquence at his command. He was warning his party and nation that the sick, slick and slimy methods of political hate-mongers and extremists could wreck the GOP and therefore the two-party system.

Although his party, made captive by the grisly Goldwater forces, did not listen, Governor Rockefeller has not given up the crusade to prove that justice and decency in politics can win the day.

A little more than a month after writing this column, Robinson told his readers that Rockefeller had hired him to be special assistant for community affairs. In his February 26 column, Robinson wrote of his hope to "do a good job for a man who, I believe, holds in his hands the key to a most important need—the strengthening of the two-party system in our country." This was one of Robinson's dreams—a political system in which no party could or would dominate the African American vote.

"There is a second reason why I want to see liberal, progressive . . . Rockefeller Republicanism triumph," Robinson added. "I shudder at the thought of the Goldwater–Bill Buckley conservatism being allowed once again to capture the Republican Party. The far-out, right-wing kooks, goons, and bigots who constituted a frightening segment of the pro-Goldwater offensive would sign the death warrant" of the progressive legacy that Abraham Lincoln left the party.[9]

9. *New York Amsterdam News,* February 26, 1966, 13.

Reagan Is Another Goldwater—but Smart

Ronald Reagan, then a candidate for governor of California, left a poor impression on Robinson, as well as many other African Americans, when he stormed out of the 1966 convention of the National Negro Republican Assembly. The purpose of the NNRA was to advance African American interests within the party, and Reagan had become incensed during a heated discussion of his views on civil rights legislation. By this point, Robinson was describing himself as a "Rockefeller Republican."[10]

Source: New York Amsterdam News, June 18, 1966, 15.

I HATE TO SAY, "I told you so."

But I did.

I've been trying to point out quite often in this column that Senator Barry Goldwater may have lost in the last national election but that Goldwaterism and John Birchism have not lost; that, in fact, the radical right and even the lunatic fringe right is making great strides in this country. They are doing it because they are willing to work and sacrifice and organize *between* elections. They are getting away with it because decent people are asleep.

The victory of Ronald Reagan in California is, in my view, a tragedy. If I read Reagan correctly, he is another Barry Goldwater—with what the kids call "smarts." I have a feeling that Mr. Goldwater is a little more honest than Mr. Reagan in his projection of his views. I have a feeling that Ronald Reagan, the actor, does a pretty skillful job of attempting to convince the public that he is all things to all men.

I may be wrong about Mr. Reagan, but there is one thing of which I am certain. If I were a voter in the state of California, I would have to ask Mr. Reagan some mighty hard questions and he would have to give me some mighty straight answers before he could get my vote. Furthermore, if

10. Robinson to John Lindsay, February 10, 1966, Nelson A. Rockefeller Papers Personal, RG 4, series P, box 16, folder 392, Rockefeller Family Archives, Rockefeller Archive Center, Sleepy Hollow, New York.

I couldn't get those answers—satisfactory answers—I would work like the devil trying to prevent Mr. Reagan's election.

I note that one of the first things that Mr. Reagan did was to call for party unity. I don't know what party unity means to Mr. Reagan. I know what it meant to Mr. Goldwater. It meant: "Look, I'm in charge now and you do it my way, see, or else . . ."

If Mr. Reagan wants unity behind his rejection of the civil rights bill to which Senator Goldwater also objected, and if he wants unity in his emphasis on the unrest in Watts rather than on a balanced evaluation of the unrest and the factors which help *bring about* the unrest—then he wouldn't be able to get me and a whole lot of other people, colored and white, to buy his unity bid.

Note to GOP: Go to Hell

Robinson suffered a heart attack on June 28, 1968, but it did not sap his energy for a full-out assault on the Republican nomination of Richard Nixon for the US presidency.
Source: New York Amsterdam News, August 17, 1968, 13.

IT IS NO LONGER A SECRET that I was immobilized by a heart attack just a few weeks back . . .

First, I want to say that I have been deeply touched and made to feel a very real sense of humble gratitude for all those who have utilized various methods of wishing me well. It is when you are sick or in trouble that you find out how many wonderful people there are in a world that sometimes seems to have gone mad with illness and trouble of a social kind.

My doctors would not permit me to attend the Republican National Convention and I suppose that was all for the best. The convention and the result—the nomination of Richard Nixon—are signs of the sick and troubled times. It was a white folks' affair and the once Grand Old Party's new caretakers, under Richard Nixon, leaned over backwards to give Dixie some Southern Comfort.

How sickening it was to hear Strom Thurmond, an arrogant little race-baiter, declaring that Mr. Nixon had promised him and the Deep South veto power over the choice of a vice-presidential candidate. . . .

Make no mistake about it—America is in peril. The talk from the backlashers about not tolerating violence means nothing. Black people are not afraid to die and there are hundreds of thousands of young black people who would rather make a last-ditch stand for freedom in the ghettos of their cities than in the jungles of Vietnam.

The lily-white nature of the GOP convention will come back to haunt it and I predict—and if I can help this prediction come true, count on me, heart trouble or not, to do so—that the same humiliating whipping that we gave Goldwater will be repeated against Nixon.

It is incredible that the GOP could be so unsensible and so stupid as not to wish to take advantage of the willingness of a man of Nelson Rockefeller's quality and courage to carry their standard. They deserve the man they got—a double-talker, a two-time loser, an adjustable man with a convertible conscience—Richard Nixon.

But black people do not deserve this, nor does America. The Republican Party has told the black man to go to hell. I offer them a similar invitation.

Nevertheless, Robinson continued to struggle to find room in the Republican Party for the remainder of his life, even attending a fund-raising event for President Nixon in 1972. His presence at this event, hosted by the Black Committee to Reelect the President, reveals not only his dissatisfaction with Senator George McGovern, the Democratic candidate whom Robinson no doubt considered weak on foreign policy, but especially his consistent practice of letting past battles remain in the past in order to advance the goal of first-class citizenship.

If there is any theme that unites many of the topics that Robinson addressed in his columns, it is this: first-class citizenship for all US citizens, especially African Americans who had long been denied the fundamental rights guaranteed by the US Constitution and the Bill of Rights.

Robinson's vision of first-class citizenship—equal justice and dignity for all—provided both the motivation and the goal not only for many of his

columns but also for his everyday life. Through his writings, and the passion-
ate actions that fueled them in public and private, Robinson himself ada-
mantly personified the first-class citizenship that he so desperately craved for
his children and for every American.

Sometimes he failed along the way. Indeed, his columns were not always
effective. African Americans, for example, never rallied around Richard
Nixon in the ways that Robinson had hoped for in his 1960 columns with
the "New York Post." But sometimes they were effective, as when his column
for the "Post" helped Charlie Sifford crack the color barrier in professional
golf, or when his column for the "New York Amsterdam News" helped to raise
fifty thousand dollars for rebuilding southern churches scorched because of
their efforts in registering African Americans to vote.

But whether his columns were effective or not, Robinson would never
give up. Echoing back to those grand moments when he stole home plate
for the Dodgers, giving rise to cheers from fans disappointed so many times
through the years, Robinson, until the day of his death in 1972, always put
his head down and made a mad dash for the goal of first-class citizenship so
that all Americans could at last stand tall and enjoy the rights and privileges
guaranteed them in the land of the free and the home of the brave. In this
sense, Robinson was not a Republican icon. He was not a Democratic icon.
Driven by the promises of democracy, Jackie Robinson was an American
icon both at and far beyond home plate.

Index